JUST LUCKY, I GUESS

Just Lucky, I Guess

BY MARY WOOD

Foreword by Ruth Lyons

Doubleday & Company, Inc., Garden City, New York, 1967

To Sally, with Love

A WORD ABOUT "MERRY MARY" *by Ruth Lyons*

To be a radio-TV columnist without resorting to personal innuendoes, half-truths, and unsubstantiated facts, and yet keep a readership that increases daily, is seemingly impossible. Yet "Merry Mary" has done just this.

I have no doubt that the longevity of her column plus her advanced age have both contributed to this achievement.

Mary is truly a great asset to the radio and television industry in Cincinnati and the surrounding territory. She has ever been outspoken without being hurtful; she has been lavish in her praise of talent when she deems it worthy; she has been accurate in her reporting and gentle in her reproof. She writes with a delightful humor about herself, her family, her friends and her late-lamented collie dog, Buster, gallant leader of the Riverside Drive Cold Nose and Marching Society, and her comments on TV commercials are hilarious. She has never poked fun at anyone without her tongue in her cheek.

In this book, Mary has gathered together a number of her various columns, written with humor, warmth and, at times, with tender reminiscence, with one idea in mind: that you may become acquainted with what we here in the Ohio Valley, through the Cincinnati *Post & Times-Star*, have the good fortune to enjoy daily.

CONTENTS

Just Lucky, I Guess

_____

Not long ago, while listening to the radio late one night, I felt a warm and sudden kinship for the announcer. He was struggling with the word "capacity," which has given me trouble for years.

"Capa . . . capa . . ." he bungled, finally emerging triumphantly with "capa-CITY," which is usually the way I mangle it unless I handle the matter with great care. I have the same problem with "macadam," which invariably comes out "mack-a-dam," and "misled," which looks like it's pronounced "MI-sled" when I see it in print.

This sorry state of affairs I blame entirely on my father, a man with a fiendish sense of humor, who, when I first came upon these words, encouraged my unique pronunciation.

My father also was responsible for a strange misconception about hotels which plagued me for years. It began during the years I attended boarding school in Millersburg, Kentucky, and traveled from Millersburg to Covington by bus.

As the bus rounded the Big Bend in the Dixie Highway, a large sign touting the Hotel Gibson loomed ahead.

"Hotel Gibson," read the sign. "No cover until 9:30 P.M."

This cryptic message, which I considered a warning, puzzled me for months. Why no covers until 9:30 P.M.? Suppose you were dead tired and simply couldn't stay awake until 9:30 P.M.? Would the Hotel Gibson relent and, perhaps, give you a thin blanket at–say–8:30 P.M.? The whole thing was completely incomprehensible to me.

I finally took the matter up with my father at breakfast one morning. Surely he, a newspaperman, would know the reason for the Hotel Gibson's chintzy policy on bedding!

As it turned out, my father said he didn't know the reason, but it was a policy he had deplored for years. Furthermore, he added, that wasn't the worst of it.

"You'll find this hard to believe, Mary Thompson, but not only do you NOT get covers until 9:30 P.M.," he told me, "they come in at five in the morning and snatch them away from you!"

The Hotel Gibson sign at the Big Bend of the Dixie Highway has been gone a long, long time. I trust this means that the Sheraton-Gibson Hotel has changed its policy on bedding!

When Cornelia Otis Skinner, on Mike Douglas' show, spoke of her mother, she revived several hilarious memories of my mother, especially the afternoon Cornelia recalled the time her mother had one of those mother-daughter chats with her to explain the facts of life. I'm sure Cornelia's mother and mine were of the same vintage —The Mauve Decade—because S-E-X was never mentioned in our family either.

I had been married for almost two years when Mamma apparently decided the time was ripe for her to break the awful truth to me. Her decision was undoubtedly prompted by the undeniable fact that I was expecting a baby in August and it was then mid-July.

The day Mamma came to call was, I'm sure, the hottest day in the summer of 1937. She was hatted and gloved. I was wearing a red-checked smock which was the only garment I could get into by then. My friends told me I resembled a brick outhouse.

"My, it's as hot as New Orleans, Mary Thompson," said Mamma, dabbing her forehead with a handkerchief which was to get quite a workout as our visit progressed. "I think I'll just have a small glass of Southern Comfort."

Being president of the United Daughters of the Confederacy, Stonewall Jackson Chapter, Mamma felt that Southern Comfort was a drink with patriotic ramifications. She was also inordinately fond of the 100-proof liquor.

Having been fortified for the ordeal, Mamma proceeded.

"Mary Thompson," she began grimly. "When a girl gets married, things change."

"What things, Mamma?" I asked innocently.

"Things," replied Mamma vaguely. "Men are different from women."

"How, Mamma?" I asked.

"I think I'll just have another little glass of Southern Comfort," she said, mopping her brow.

She took that one in one gulp and forged ahead.

"Although Chip is not a southern boy, I like him," said Mamma, "but he is a man. I want you to know that."

"I do," I said. "You just told me."

"What I mean is that when a girl gets married, things are liable to happen," she said desperately.

Although I was enjoying our little tête-à-tête to the hilt, I could see that Mamma wasn't.

"Look, Mamma, are you trying to tell me that I'm pregnant?" I asked bluntly. Mamma turned ashen.

"Oh, Mary Thompson, NEVER use that word!" she practically sobbed. "Just say you're in a family way!"

"Well, whatever you want to call it, Mamma, you've come too late," I pointed out.

So, after another belt of Southern Comfort, Mamma went away with the satisfaction of a distasteful job well done and the supreme confidence that the word P-R-E-G-N-A-N-T would never again sully the lips of her only daughter.

Almost everyone has a personal ghost story and so have I. It's a sad, tender little story which I remember vividly now, although it made little impression on me at the time it happened. I was very young then—seven, as I recall —and I suppose children accept such things as a matter of course; there are so many things they don't understand.

In those days I lived with my mother and grandmother in a rambling old house in New Orleans, on Valence Street, just off St. Charles Avenue.

I'm sure I was fond of my mother, but it is my grandmother who stands out in my memory. She was my best friend. I adored her, and recall so many things about her: her fascinating stories of New Orleans during the Civil War; her humor and great understanding; the delicate odor of her perfume—Violet Sec—that always seemed to cling to her. We were practically inseparable and even shared the same old-fashioned four-poster bed, which was covered by a tester from which hung voluminous folds of white mosquito netting.

My grandmother was one of a large family that had lived in the Mississippi Delta. My great-grandfather, a wealthy sugar planter until the war, had sired twenty children by two wives. Of all her many sisters, my grand-

mother's favorite was Ida, several years her senior. Aunt
Ida, whom Grandmother always called "Sister Ida" was
now living on a plantation near Lake Charles, Louisiana,
and although they visited back and forth frequently, they
wrote each other every day.

As I remember, Grandmother had just returned from
a visit with Aunt Ida when, several nights later, Aunt
Ida paid her last visit to us—from the spirit world.

It must have been past midnight when I was awakened
by my grandmother's voice. She was sitting up in bed,
talking to someone who was invisible to me. Whoever it
was apparently stood at the foot of our bed. There must
have been moonlight streaming into the room because I
remember exactly how Grandmother looked. She was
wearing a long cambric nightgown with high ruffled neck
and long sleeves and, of course, her beruffled nightcap.

I knew my grandmother wasn't frightened, but I knew
she was very sad. I could hear only her end of the conversation, but I soon realized that she was talking to Aunt
Ida and that Aunt Ida was asking her to do certain
things.

"Yes, Sister Ida, I understand," I can recall hearing
Grandmother saying. "You want Ida May to have your
garnet cross and the Paisley shawl."

There were other instructions, but that particular one
stands out in my memory because Ida May was my
mother and she, in turn, left the garnet cross to me. I still
have it.

Grandmother and Aunt Ida must have talked for about
ten minutes. Then the time came for them to say
good-by. Only then did tears begin to stream down my
grandmother's face.

"Good-by, Sister Ida," she whispered brokenly, "I shall miss you very much."

Then she lay back in bed and told me, quietly and unemotionally, that Aunt Ida had just passed away and had come to say good-by. I don't recall being frightened in the least, just sleepy.

The next morning a telegram came telling of Aunt Ida's death of a heart attack. She had died suddenly, just before midnight.

I saw Cousin Louie on television the other night and I thought, "Now there's a cat who has sure come a long way from Rampart Street." And then I got to thinking about the days when Cousin Louie was the hottest tailgater ever to accompany a funeral procession down Valence Street in New Orleans, on the way to the colored cemetery about a half-mile down the road.

It was years before I found out that Cousin Louie's last name was Armstrong. Back in those days he was our cook Mattie's Cousin Louie.

I suppose Burial Societies in New Orleans have gone the way of the horse-drawn hearse—an impressive vehicle in which to take your last ride—but when I was a small, adenoidal lass on Valence Street, the Burial Societies put on the grandest, noisiest funeral processions ever known.

Granted, the degree of grandeur and noise depended upon how much burial insurance the departed had managed to acquire before shuffling off the mortal coil, but a really bang-up procession was a thing of joy to behold and hear, especially to the kids in our neighborhood.

The word would spread like a grass fire down Valence Street that the burying parade had just turned off St. Charles Avenue and for blocks around we kids would drop whatever devilment we were up to and rush to meet it.

First would come, in full regalia, the fellow members of the Burial Society, marching in solemn splendor and usually bearing aloft a banner proclaiming, "Death Where Is Thy Sting?" Then would come the mourners—some genuine, some paid recruits and some who just came along for the music. The hearse, horse-drawn, came next, and last, but most important, came the tail-gate band. The number of musicians in the band was in direct proportion to the departed's insurance.

Cousin Louie, because of his tremendous volume and apparent inexhaustibility, was in great demand for these occasions. Naturally, Mattie was loathe to miss one of her talented cousin's performances and I was dispatched to scout the procession and hotfoot it back with the word.

"Cousin Louie's blowing the horn, Mattie," I'd holler with what breath I had left, and off we'd go like bats out of hell to join the procession.

As the parade made its slow, mournful progress to the graveyard the music was fittingly somber. Usually, we had a choice of "Swing Low, Sweet Chariot" or "When the Saints Come Marching In." It may come as a surprise to the Dixieland cultist, but "The Saints" was a funeral march long before it became their theme song.

By the time the procession had reached its destination quite a large group had been assembled. We would wait patiently until the departed had been laid to rest because then came the moment we'd waited for—the marching back.

It was then that Cousin Louie cut loose, leading the band through chorus after chorus of "Oh, Didn't He

Ramble" or a spirited rendition of "Milenberg Joys" as the mourners and spectators alike cavorted down the street in joyous abandon.

They just don't have funerals like that any more but I'm mighty glad I was around when they did.

My favorite small boy on television will always be Beaver Cleaver (Jerry Mathers) of "Leave It to Beaver." Although I never was a small boy, the Beaver and I have much in common stashed away in my fast-dimming memory.

We both have nurtured baby alligators in the bathtub—I still recall my mother's piercing shriek—and we both sold perfume from door to door.

Beaver's venture into the perfume business was prompted by a desire to win a movie projector. I was going to be rewarded with a pony.

I often wonder how many other trusting ten-year-olds were beguiled by that enchanting "Win a Pony of Your Own" ad and, having answered it, found themselves the neighborhood representative for Radio Girl Perfume.

The manufacturers of Radio Girl Perfume—whose generosity was exceeded only by the stench of their product—sent a free bottle of perfume, along with the two dozen to be sold, so the junior saleswoman could douse herself liberally.

It was the free sample that blasted my career as a purveyor of perfume. My father had a very sensitive nose.

"Something's died in here! What is it?" he shouted when he came in the front door.

"It's Mary Thompson," said Mamma. "She's going to win a pony."

"But does she have to smell like a goat?" asked my father.

The details of my business venture were carefully explained to my father, along with the envisioned acquisition of a pony.

"Why does she want a pony?" my father demanded. "She's already got a cat."

"She can't ride a cat to school," said Mamma.

"Why not? He's the biggest damn cat I ever saw," said Father.

Well, the perfume was shipped back the next day, including the one bottle I'd sold our cook. She was glad to get her money back after she smelled the Radio Girl.

I took a bath by request.

Cincinnati's beautiful and historic May Festival and the May Festival produced by the Millersburg Female College Glee Club have nothing in common except the title, but often during the merry month of May, my memory wanders back to May 1930, when the damsels of the Millersburg Female College Glee Club took to the hills of Kentucky to cut a wide swathe of song and culture through Paintsville, Prestonsburg, Catlettsburg and other communities with our one-night May Festival stands.

I wouldn't say that any of the young ladies, ranging in age from fifteen to eighteen, were over-loaded with vocal talents, but we had rehearsed assiduously all year and, at least, knew the words to all the selections, which included "Welcome, Sweet Springtime, We Greet Thee With Song," "The Bells of St. Mary's," and Friml's "The Bubble Song." What we lacked in tone, we made up in volume of sound.

So early that May, accompanied by our Glee Club director, Mrs. Gibson, and Dr. R. H. Holliday, president of Millersburg Female College and affectionately known as "Uncle Horsecollar," we boarded a venerable bus and headed for the hills.

Disaster followed disaster on that tour, but our first

day out was beset by only minor mishaps. Ogreeta Holliday got carsick all over the balloons which figured prominently in our big production number, "Float On, Float On, Oh Bubbles of Rainbow Hue," and we had to stop in Morehead to get new ones.

At Ashland we were enthusiastically received by members of the Epworth League who plied us with strawberry shortcake, causing our soprano, Leota Kelly, to break out in hives.

Paintsville, being Alpharetta Butcher's home town, left no stone unturned in demonstrating its hospitality, even to giving a dance for the young ladies. Unfortunately, some of our dancing partners suffered a malady known as "Jake Leg" and were unable to trip the light fantastic.

It wasn't until we hit Prestonsburg that it was discovered the electric iron had been left behind in Millersburg. Blame for this misfortune rested squarely on the shoulders of Elgiva Clark, who owned the only iron in school and made a small fortune renting it out at ten cents an hour.

But the show must go on, as they say, so clad in bedraggled, beruffled organdy dresses of rainbow hue, the young ladies of the Millersburg Female College Glee Club greeted Sweet Springtime once again in voices so shrill it made your back teeth ache.

As I look back on our Prestonsburg concert, Walpurgis Night pales by comparison. Rabbit Anderson, who rang the bells in "The Bells of St. Mary's," misplaced the bells at the last minute and sobbed as only Rabbit could sob throughout our entire rendition. Leota Kelly's organdy dress irritated her hives, acquired earlier in Ashland, so she scratched as she sang. And Ogreeta Holliday could be clearly heard huffing and puffing as she blew up the balloons for our big Dixie Finish production number, "The Bubble Song."

It was, regrettably, "The Bubble Song" which gave the coup de grâce to the final performance of the Millersburg Female College Glee Club's May Festival in Prestonsburg. As the young ladies tripped daintily on-stage in their rumpled organdy, each held aloft a balloon. This was too much temptation for a small boy in the front row whose parents had failed to separate him from his BB gun before the concert.

The first BB hit Leota, causing her to stop scratching and leap into the air. That kid was a whiz. Direct hit followed direct hit and the damsels fled the stage in complete rout.

That was the last May Festival ever produced by the Millersburg Female College Glee Club, but "The Bubble Song" will remain forever green in our memories.

If "General Hospital" or "The Doctors" ever run low on afflictions, I have a humdinger for them: My Seven-Year Itch.

Not only will I contribute the script but I'll gladly act as the case in point.

A number of my former schoolmates from Millersburg Female College, which once graced Millersburg, Kentucky, will be happy to join me, I'm sure. We scratched it out in two semesters, but, my, it was a busy two semesters.

Nobody was ever quite certain how the daughters of some of the better Bluegrass families became afflicted with The Itch, but it spread through our institution of learning and culture like a grass fire.

Our dean, Miss Elizabeth Brown, became extremely suspicious when she first noticed an undue amount of twitching among her charges during our frequent church attendance. She was further alarmed, at our social gatherings, to see us make numberless trips behind the potted palms—WITHOUT the boys.

It was old Doc Calhoun, a man who had treated everything from delirium tremens to hog-bite, who finally diagnosed our misery.

"Elizabeth," he said, "those girls have got the goldurndest case of The Itch I ever did see. It sure is gonna be hell to cure."

He then ordered several gallons of a particularly odoriferous sulphur ointment and plastered the victims with it from head to toe.

Distressed and horrified at having a school full of frantically scratching damsels, Miss Brown called an emergency chapel meeting to explain to us our embarrassing plight.

"Young ladies," she urged in closing, "let us keep this our little secret. I don't think our parents would be pleased to learn of our little trouble."

So we kept "our little secret" all through our visit home during Christmas vacation. But several weeks later most of our families were actively sharing it.

I still remember the special-delivery letter I received from my mother several months later, after I'd written that I would soon be home for spring vacation.

Mamma's letter was brief and to the point:

"For the love of God, Mary Thompson, DON'T come home," she wrote. "We just got your father cured of The Itch!"

When I think of the many and wondrous ways television has enriched my life, I can hardly fight back the tears of gratitude. I might have gone through life smelling different from every other woman if Arlene Francis hadn't made it pretty plain that any female worth her chic should be reeking of Arpège.

And I wouldn't be caught dead in the wrong girdle, either. If I'm going to be caught dead, it will be in a girdle I'll be proud to be caught dead in. Not one that will have me twitching in my coffin.

But it wasn't until just the other day that I stumbled upon the true secret of glorious hair . . . champagne!

It was on my favorite afternoon peek at how the other half lives, "Here's Hollywood," that I learned this simple, everyday beauty tip of which I have been so shamefully ignorant, and I want to thank Arlene Dahl, who enlightened me.

Arlene said that Greer Garson always rinses her hair in champagne.

"It doesn't have to be imported champagne," Arlene explained. "Domestic is just as good."

As a matter of fact, Arlene said, just any old champagne you happen to have left over in the refrigerator will do.

Isn't that heavenly, girls. We don't have to worry about the vintage or the proper temperature, or even hollow-stemmed glasses. Just use what's left of that bottle of scrubbing champagne you had with last night's pheasant, so it shouldn't be a total loss.

See what I mean about TV enriching my life? I shudder to think of the wasted nights I've spent drinking champagne when I could have been washing my hair. You can bet I'll never make that mistake again!

All this has left me with one minor dilemma which Arlene failed to clear up. If I want to have my hair done properly from now on, do I go to a bar?

Reading Jessica Mitford's book *The American Way of Death,* on the burial business, brought back vivid memories of my early days on the *Post.* I wrote obituaries, but not for long. My lifelong affliction terminated my brief career as an obit writer.

My affliction is over-active tear ducts. I go to the movies and cry at the coming attractions. The mere sight of dear little Shirley Temple, Lassie or Mimi's death scene in *La Bohème* breaks me up. Worst of all, when anyone else cries, I join in wholeheartedly.

The job of an obit writer entails phoning the bereaved for information about the deceased. This is where I bogged down. If the bereaved wept, I wept. Although I might never have heard of or set eyes upon their Loved One, I was a veritable Wailing Wall. By the time I'd made four or five calls, my eyes were so swollen I could barely see to type the obit.

I must say that the bereaved were deeply touched by my involuntary emotion. My editor, the late Carl Groat, received a steady stream of letters congratulating him upon employing such a tender-hearted young woman.

My free time was spent trotting from one funeral home

to another, visiting people who had died before I ever met them because I'd become a family friend over the phone.

My most disastrous visit, however, had nothing to do with my obit writing. The mother of a friend had died and I set out to pay a condolence call at the funeral home.

Sobbing softly, I was ushered over to the casket, looked down and was horrified to see an elderly gentleman—a total stranger to me. I knew at once I'd gone to the wrong funeral home, but since I was crying harder than anyone else in the room, the baffled relatives assumed I must have been very close to the old gentleman. Perhaps, they thought, some mysterious woman out of his past.

My embarrassment was acute, especially since I couldn't seem to turn off the freshet of tears I'd started. The relatives were equally embarrassed because nobody knew who I was. Several people patted my back and one man offered his handkerchief.

"You'll be with us tomorrow, of course," whispered a middle-aged woman, probably a daughter.

"If I can bear it," I sobbed, groping my way to the door and thence to the right funeral home.

I've often speculated on the questions the family must have asked each other concerning my identity.

"The brazen hussy, coming right to the funeral home," I can hear one of the ladies saying. "And we always thought Papa was such a devoted family man!"

As I was planting petunias the other day, nattily clad in an elderly pair of bluejeans and my daughter Sally's old Denison sweat shirt; our friendly mailman arrived with another urgent message from *Vogue* magazine's Katherine Osgood, saying that what was chic for last season may be out-of-date almost as soon as I had received my very first compliment.

Since I hadn't received my very first compliment on what I was wearing, I felt compelled to read on. Where had I gone wrong? Did Miss Osgood have the answer?

Indeed she did! Why wasn't I wearing a shoulder-to-floor torrent of chinchilla, wrapped on the horizontal? For only $13,000 I could wear it evenings at home like a dishabille.

Once I am swathed in this torrent of chinchilla, this is no time to quit in my relentless quest for chic. What I need now is a tiger lily for my hair—a mere $125—which is rhinestone-spotted with a pear-shaped bogus-pearl center.

Are you out of your mind, Miss Osgood? With that chinchilla bathrobe how can you expect me to wear anything less than diamonds and real pearls?

Anyone as avant-garde as I shall certainly be, stumbling down Riverside Drive, ablaze with diamonds and tripping over chinchilla, has simply got to have an avant-garde pet, I can assure you. And Miss Osgood has just the pet for me.

"Hark back to the days of Cleopatra with a descendant of the sacred cats of Egypt—an Abyssinian," advises Miss Osgood.

To be honest, I had almost despaired of becoming the woman Miss Osgood and *Vogue* expect me to be until I came upon their tip on "new things to do with vodka."

"Mix the East Side," Miss Osgood suggested. "Crush fresh mint with a half teaspoon of sugar, add a jigger of vodka, juice of half a lime, ice, shake well and radiate."

Madam, I lost no time . . . and, Man, did I radiate!

Word has reached me in Hollywood that cancer has killed Candy Newman and, I know, broken the hearts of her mother and father. To lose a child is the deepest of all tragedies to any parent. But to lose a beloved only daughter just beginning her adult life—Candy was twenty-one —is grief beyond compare.

Candy was a sweet, shy, gentle girl whose life was filled with love. Her parents, Ruth and Herman, were very close to her, and she was happiest at home with them and with the dogs and cats she loved. I remember, when Candy was a little girl, she wanted to be a veterinarian because of her love for animals.

Throughout the year and a half since she was stricken by that vicious malignancy, Candy's courage has been unbelievable. After the first operation, when her breast was removed, Candy comforted her heart-broken parents by saying: "I didn't want to be a Playboy Club Bunny, anyway."

Candy loved to travel and wanted very much to take the European trip from which she never returned.

There are things which happen that will never be understood. Why should this shattering blow be dealt to

Ruth, who has tirelessly devoted her energies to making other people's children happy?

Ruth's world revolved around the daughter she loved so much. They were more than mother and daughter, they were dear companions who shared everything—laughter, jokes, interests and tears. I don't know how Ruth has gotten through these last months, knowing what Candy didn't know—that there was no hope—and putting up a brave front for the child she knew she would soon lose forever.

There are no words I can say or write which could possibly take away the anguish and emptiness that Ruth and Herman are going through now and for years to come. I only hope they will be comforted by the memory of the love and happiness they gave that wonderful child for all of her twenty-one years with them.

Some people think writing a TV column is the softest job devised since bingo callers became in great demand.

Well, allow me to dispel this illusion. There are times when, in the interest of my readers, I have risen in misery to see a TV show and Saturday morning was one of those times.

Having attended a particularly joyous festivity Friday night, it was painful to recall that I had promised Dave Manning I would watch his new small-fry show, "Mr. Hop," at 8:30 A.M. Saturday.

As I tried to focus my eyes on the large white rabbit leaping about the TV screen, I shuddered.

"It's Harvey," I groaned. "He's come back to haunt me."

It wasn't Harvey, I soon discovered. It was Mr. Hop, the Magic Bunny, who hangs out in a toy shop with Alex, the Court Jester, and a bunch of wooden soldiers, and he had all sorts of goodies in store for me that morning if I could just remember the magic words.

The only magic words I could recall were: "Let's have one for the road!"

Pretty soon along came a cartoon about this nosy elf who made a pair of shoes for an old shoemaker and almost drove the poor soul out of his mind trying to guess who made the shoes. This cliffhanger will be continued next week.

It wasn't long before Mr. Hop said he was going to introduce me to an old friend and whom did I think he was? Did I have any idea who would be there? Well, it would be my old friend Santa Claus and I should ask him to bring me a Schmoo Game for Christmas.

Schmoo Game? Just let him come down my chimney with a Schmoo Game and I'll clout him with it. What I want is a brand new head!

But kidding aside, Dave, it's a cute show . . . especially if you're five years old and drink nothing but milk!

Between television and a childhood misspent at the neighborhood picture show (remember when we called 'em that?) watching cowboys and Indians, I've become a reasonably sound authority on Westerns. Just show me the first reel and I'll have the plot and characters pegged.

I have learned over the years, for example, that only the horse is trustworthy. People, in Westerns, are no darn good. Even the hero can turn on you, if you don't look pretty sharp.

What never ceases to undo me is how the hero can be so all-fired stupid. He rides into a town with his rugged countenance shining with good will toward men. Right away, usually in the saloon, he meets his dead father's old friend. Dead Dad's Old Friend springs for a couple of belts of Bonded Sani-Flush and quick as a wink, Our Hero figures he has nothing more to worry about because Dead Dad's Old Friend is now his lifelong pal.

That will be the day! Beware Dead Dad's Old Friend, especially if he is a banker. Watch out for them bankers.

Along about the second reel—after he gets out of the saloon—Our Hero probably will meet and fall for the Town Belle. Now he is in big trouble because her father hates him. What's more, Town Belle is so dumb she is bound to louse up Our Hero just by accident. She has a big mouth and tells everything she knows to the banker.

I have found that you seldom run into a bad bartender in a Western. These fellows hear a lot, but they ain't loud-mouths. They are extremely adept at dodging bullets, so they almost never get shot. Matter of fact, shooting a bar-tender is like shooting a horse. It just isn't done.

My editor, Dick Thornburg, is a Western watcher of long standing. He insists that he has seen funerals on Westerns and that the mortally wounded villains don't just litter up the main street. I have not, although on several occasions I have caught a glimpse of the town undertaker, looking very prosperous.

It's true that Westerns have changed a lot since the days when my mother urged me to spend Saturday after-noon at the neighborhood picture show. In those days, it wasn't too difficult to tell the good guys from the bad. The bad guys always wore black hats.

Nowadays, it isn't that easy. There isn't anyone pure bad or pure good any more. Even the meanest killer is just some poor, misunderstood lad whose Pappy whupped him for setting fire to his little sister.

But if you're contemplating riding into a western town to reclaim the ranch your dear old dad was skunked out of, here are some ground rules to follow: Drink your whisky straight and alone. Pay the bartender in Confeder-ate money. And don't tell the sheriff your right name.

You might get lynched, but at least you won't have your faith in your fellow man shattered!

Nothing brings out the Mother-Loved-Me-but-She-Died brand of wallowing self-pity in me like a good, old-fashioned cold in the head. Who cares whether I live or die except those lovely people on TV whose aching sinus cavities are filled with sponges, as are mine: whose eyes are watering, whose noses are red and dripping like faucets and who would be better off dead?

They were my only friends over the weekend. The only ones I could really count on. Nobody else would touch me with a ten-foot pole.

But let me tell you of the people I grew to hate as I sat huddled in my old woolly bathrobe, sneezing and wheezing, awaiting the Grim Reaper who was looking less and less grim. It was those dames, blooming with health, who kept telling me how to be glamorous.

Glamorous, flamorous! I'm lucky to be here at all, let alone slather my face with Noxema (forehead, chin and both cheeks) so my complexion will be petal-soft in a week. So who is my complexion going to be petal-soft for—the undertaker?

And how about I should douse myself with Chanel No. 5? I can't smell anything and, anyway, even Chanel

No. 5 would have a tough time competing with the overpowering aroma of Vick's Vatronol nose drops.

I find soap operas of inestimable solace to one on the verge of departing this Vale of Tears via a head cold. No matter how low you have sunk, these people have sunk lower—in spades. It's the kind of dependable chronic misery you can rely upon. By the grace of God, your nose may stop running and your troubles will be over. Not theirs. For them, nothing is so bad today that it can't get worse tomorrow!

Take my old chums on "The Secret Storm." You may recall, last spring, that we really had a time with dear little Amy Ames. Her grand passion for her college professor, unfortunately married at the time, resulted in a slight touch of pregnancy which progressed to the Ames' Clan's widespread agony. The college professor departed into the wild blue yonder but, happily, Amy had an old beau warming up in the bull pen. That was Kip who had gotten out of jail just in time to marry her and avert dire calamity.

You would think, wouldn't you, that dear little Amy's troubles would be over for the time being, at least. Don't you kid yourself. There's a new girl in town named Janet —she's the daughter of the lady who just wed Amy's father—who is pretending to be Amy's best friend but who, in reality, is well on her way to snatching Amy's husband, Kip.

How about that, Redleg fans!

I may be a sick, tired, old lady, but I know a female snake when I see one. And that Janet is a female snake with her cap set in all directions. Now that she's split the blanket with Jerry (that's Amy's brother), Kip is next on her list.

It's quite obvious that Janet has been watching all those TV commercials which insure 100 per cent glamor. When Kip calls on her for a little tea and sympathy, she gives him both barrels—candlelight, soft, romantic music (those Jackie Gleason albums which have gotten too many guys in trouble), a seductive, satin hostess gown and, Heaven forfend, BOOZE!

Janet is now making the martinis nine to one and telling Kip that Amy is simply not emotionally equipped to understand the deep sensitivity of his soul. God only knows what will happen next, but if I can keep this blasted cold going for another couple of weeks I'll find out.

Crosley Square is celebrating Paul Dixon's tenth anniversary on Channel 5 today (April 23, 1965), and I am celebrating a twenty-year friendship with one of the nicest, warmest people in broadcasting.

Dear Paul, is it possible that twenty years have gone by since you and Marge hove into town on a rainy Christmas Day, driving a car with a leaky roof and with seven dollars in your pocket?

Paul and I became friends when he was broadcasting WCPO news from a reclaimed broom closet in the old *Post* building and I had just begun writing this column. We'd have coffee together every morning and Dixon would bewail his job as a newscaster.

"Mary, I'm the world's worst newscaster. I'm a cheerful guy and I just can't sound like the world's coming to an end every hour on the hour," he'd moan. "If I could just talk Mort Watters into giving me a disc jockey show, I'd be the happiest man alive."

Shortly thereafter it dawned on Mr. Watters that the world's worst newscaster might possibly be the world's best disc jockey. He gave Paul a show and within months Dixon had the town by the ears, so to speak. To quote an old column of mine: "To teen-agers he's the man

they want to marry, and to middle-aged matrons, he's
the man they should have married." Back in the mid-
forties, Paul was the local equivalent of all the Beatles
rolled into one.

In 1949, when WCPO-TV went on the air, Watters
informed Paul that, as the town's leading disc jockey, he
was to be favored with a two-hour television show.

"Big deal," replied Dixon. "What do I do? Spin records
for two hours every day?"

Since nobody knew any more about TV than Paul did,
he decided to just wing it and "The Paul Dixon Show"
took off.

"I remembered three guys I'd seen in a Chicago night
club," Paul recalled. "They were dressed as the Andrews
Sisters and they pantomimed their records."

To augment the record pantomiming, Paul got a pretty
teen-ager who worked in the station's record library,
Dotty Mack, to join the show. A few months later, Wanda
Lewis came to WCPO-TV to help her husband, Al, in the
art department. She was immediately pressed into service
on the Dixon show to draw sketches as the records played.

The popularity of Paul's afternoon TV show was nothing short of sensational. Here's a quote from a column I
wrote in 1950:

"Currently the bulk of the afternoon TV audience goes
to Paul Dixon's two-hour record and nonsense program.
This leaves all the experts who predicted that nobody
could click with a record show on television in a most
embarrassing dilemma. And to complicate their dilemma,
the experts can't even put their finger on WHY he clicks.

"With no production and even less rehearsal, Paul and
his two beautifully-constructed female aides, Dotty and

Wanda, seem to have hit the video jackpot. Call it slap-happy, unpredictable or whatever you want, the fact remains that it is amusing to watch, mainly because of Dixon's unquenchable good-humor and self-confidence. He seems to convey the impression that his show is a gay neighborhood party and he's glad you could come to it."

Fifteen years later, on Channel 5's morning show, Dixon's good humor is still unquenchable and he's making more friends than ever since his show is now seen in Dayton, Columbus and Indianapolis.

So congratulations on your anniversary, Paul. This town owes you a deep debt of gratitude for the countless hours of fun and frolic you've provided us.

This fool and her money went to Latonia Race Track with Leo Underhill one day this week.

"Honey, I am gonna make you so rich, you'll be buried in a silver coffin," said Leo, who lies a lot. Why he is working at WNOP instead of following his natural avocation as a race track tout, I shall never know.

So, with the grocery money clutched in my hot hand and visions of full-length sable coats dancing before my eyes, we took off at high noon. Post time is 1 P.M., which gives Leo enough time to recover from his hangover at the bar and read the Racing Form. This is serious business with Leo. You'd think he was doping the next presidential election.

As we went down the drain on the Daily Double, my vision of full-length sable coats shrank to a mink jacket. I refused Leo's kind offer to invest my money in a horse in the second race.

"This horse," Leo assured me, "will be six miles south of Lexington while the rest of those dogs are getting out of the starting gate."

"This Horse" came in biting the tail of the second last horse!

Part of the grocery money made a comeback on Tennessee Tom, but in the next race, the horse that Leo insisted he wouldn't even bet counterfeit money on, raced home paying something like 80 to 1. Leo admitted it was a slight oversight on his part and pointed out that "you can't win 'em all."

"That is the understatement of the day," I replied acidly.

The afternoon was waning fast and so was the grocery money. At the rate we were going, I would be lucky to be buried in a burlap sack after I died of starvation. About that time, Leo looked into his crystal ball (he'd abandoned the Racing Form) and came up with a horse name of The Wart.

"We've got this horse to win, place and show," he said. "Which do you want your money on?"

Being the Big Plunger of all time, I took the show ticket. The Wart sped to the finish line like a bat out of hell, paying an astronomical price to win.

And there I sat with a piccalo and my show ticket!

"Well," said Leo, "I did my best for you. Some people just don't deserve to be buried in a silver coffin."

Some days just seem to start out better than others. Such was the morning I returned to my desk from Hollywood and found a brochure urging me to "Be A Playboy Club Bunny."

"Enjoy a glamorous career as you make top earnings at the world-famous Playboy Club," wooed this enticing communiqué.

I lost no time getting my friend Ruth Lyons on the phone.

"Get down to Crosley Square as fast as you can and hand in your resignation," I told her. "We've been wasting our time all these years. The Playboy Club is clamoring for our services. They want us to be Bunnies."

There was a momentary gasp on the other end of the line, but she recovered.

"The Hollywood sun has addled what brains you have," replied Mother.

"I kid you not, dear girl, they're panting for us," I said. "Why, it says here: 'An exciting new life awaits you as a Playboy Club Bunny. You'll never be bored by routine. You'll earn far more than other girls. You'll meet internationally famous people in show business, sports, politics, industry and finance in the glamorous and exciting atmosphere of the luxurious Playboy Clubs.'"

"Wow!" she hollered. "When do I get my ears?"

"It's only a matter of time," I said. "It so happens we both more than meet all the requirements—striking good looks, charm, intelligence, a friendly personality and cheerfulness."

"You're absolutely right," said Ruth. "Nobody can say we're not cheerful. What else?"

"Well, it seems they want us to be between eighteen and twenty-five," I said.

"That's no problem," she said airily. "We'll just do what we've been doing for years—lie."

"There's one more hurdle," I said. "They want references."

There was a long pause in our conversation while we both wondered who, in the wildest stretch of the imagination, would give us references.

"What a pity to have to turn in our ears before we even get 'em," sobbed my broken-hearted chum.

"It is a crushing blow," I replied, "but at least we know that Hugh Hefner wanted us!"

Each time I try to lend a helping hand to nature, it usually turns out to be Disasterville for both of us. You take Tuesday afternoon, for instance. I was sitting out in the back yard of Little-Tottering-on-the-Brink-of-the-Ohio, cultivating the tan I acquired at no small expense in the Caribbean and listening to that nut Jerry Thomas on the radio, when a baby bird fell out of a nest in the apple tree. Naturally it fell in my lap—where else?

Best I explain that several families of robins have taken up residence in the apple tree and also a nearby maple. One is a widow-lady whose husband recently expired on the front lawn, leaving her a family to feed alone. This has caused us both much anguish, so I keep watering the lawn to coax the earthworms to the surface. I know it's a low blow to the earthworms, but those kids have got to eat.

Well, I had barely recovered from the shock of having a naked baby bird plopped in my lap, when I realized that overhead all hell had broken loose. The lady robin and all her friends were emitting loud lamentations, apparently blaming me for the disaster.

"Look, girls, I didn't kick this kid out of the nest,

honest," I explained feverishly. "Just tell me what to do, and I'll do it."

To complicate matters, two neighboring cats who vie for my affections, bounded into the back yard, thereby increasing the ladies' lamentations.

I now have one naked baby robin, two cats hungrily eyeing baby robin, a growing force of irate lady robins and Jerry Thomas and Bob Jones doing a madly improbable interview with Gentleman Jim Corbett and his mother on the radio!

"A fine time to make me laugh," I hissed at the disembodied voices of Messrs. Thomas and Jones. "Why can't you give me some advice I can use—like how to get a bird back in a nest?"

Hotly pursued by the cats, I did manage to make it into the kitchen with the bird, slamming the door in their twitching whiskers. I then arranged the bird in a nest of cotton on a paper plate, putting a couple of drops of brandy on the cotton in the hope of reviving the patient. As an afterthought I took a small slug of brandy to revive myself.

I want to tell you, friends, that not even the most dedicated bird-lover—which after Tuesday I am not—is going to stand under a tree, holding a bird on a paper plate for more than twenty minutes. Especially with a bunch of ungrateful, loudmouth birds blaming her for the whole ugly mess.

I did what any other sensible person would have done. I got a stepladder, climbed up that tree and put the plate on a limb. It turned out those birds didn't give a hoot about that poor child. What they wanted was the brandy!

For some obscure reason—just lucky, I guess—each time my friend Bud Thoma and I seek to immerse ourselves in culture at the Zoo Opera, it turns out to be the hottest night of the summer. This probably accounts for the fact that I've seen the third acts of almost no operas.

It happened again last Friday when we attended a performance of *The Tales of Hoffmann*. The mercury, as usual, had reached an all-summer high and the Zoo Opera Pavilion could be best described as a large Turkish bath with fully dressed patrons.

On stage, which had to be hotter than the pavilion, Poet Hoffmann and friends were quaffing liberally in the neighborhood saloon as Hoffmann sang his heart out about his ill-fated amours.

"What is this you have gotten me into?" I asked Bud. "*Peyton Place* set to music?"

"I'm a stranger here myself," replied Bud, mopping his brow.

Well, Hoffmann should have stayed in that saloon where he had a few friends, because in the next act he gets himself involved with a life-size mechanical doll, the creation of an evil genius, which is smashed to pieces just about the time poor old Hoffmann thinks he has found his true love. I'm afraid that cat Hoffmann was a little near-sighted. Even I could tell she was a doll.

Since I live a reasonably sheltered life with the television programs, I was not quite prepared for Hoffmann's amour No. 2. She was a courtesan reclining on the couch of her lush palace in Venice, surrounded by admirers, including one who resembled a porcupine. He was bouncing around on the floor at her feet, nibbling on her finger tips.

"What's that?" I inquired of Bud.

"That's her dog," he informed me.

"It's the most affectionate dog I ever saw," I replied. "Anyway, it says in the program that it's an admirer."

"So it's an admiring dog," hissed Bud.

After considerable hanky-pank and vocal argument, Hoffmann lost patience and stabbed another fellow who was hanging around and not getting half the attention the lady was bestowing on her admiring dog, or whatever he was.

I will never know how Hoffmann fared with his third love because, by then, I figured this fellow was a loser with mighty strange taste in dames, and there was no point in sitting in a Turkish bath watching him go down the drain for the third time.

We spent the third act at the Playboy Club, which is air-cooled—as are the Bunnies! If Hoffmann had had his wits about him, he'd have been there, too.

Christmas is a joyous season to most people, but it brings nothing but frustration and misery to me. It is the time of the year when I am called upon to wrap gifts for my friends and loved ones.

I don't mind shopping for the gifts. I am a strong, healthy female who can get in there and slug with the best of 'em. But getting them wrapped in neat, tidy packages is another story. I was born with five thumbs on each hand.

Vainly do I pour over magazines and TV commercials illustrating how to wrap gifts attractively, emblazoned with fluffy bows and all that jazz. I try—heaven knows, I try—and the net result is a package which the recipient eyes with sheer horror, tempted to soak it in a bucket of water before opening just in case a mad bomber might be loose in the city.

Over the years I have invested a small fortune in paper, ready-made bows, glue and scotch tape. According to the simple—and I use the term loosely—directions in the numberless booklets I have also acquired, any fool can emerge triumphant with packages so glorious to behold that they would stir the soul of Michelangelo.

Well, I'm the fool that can't!

The gaily-colored paper is invariably too small for the package I want to wrap. If it fits, and this seldom happens, it mysteriously tears. The glue and scotch tape, which I apply liberally, stick only to me. Bows either immediately wilt or unravel at the mere touch of my fingers.

I might add that my rare talent for botching up gifts also extends to decorating Christmas trees. For years, I fought the annual battle of the Yule Tree valiantly. It was always a losing fight. The lights, which finally worked the year before, never lit the following year. Those fancy balls had all lost the little hooks and never, never did the blasted tree ever fit into the holder.

On several occasions, the tree—decorated through sweat and tears—toppled over and lay prone on the living room floor through the holiday. At these times, I simply explained to curious visitors that I just happened to like horizontal Christmas trees.

Since any hall I attempt to deck is likely to resemble a Charles Addams cartoon, I have settled for a couple of red candles this year. As for my friends and loved ones, I only hope they'll be happy with those nice, neat, unwrapped boxes the stuff came in.

Word has seeped through to me that Ruth Lyons has chosen Peter Grant as her matrimonial target for Leap Year 1957, and I have only one bit of advice for Pete: Take to the hills, buddy! Before another day passes, friend, head for high ground!

Let us not forget what happened to a few of Mother's earlier victims. Poor old Arthur Chandler, Jr.—after years of ceaseless harassment—finally turned in his raccoon coat and headed for South America, leaving no forwarding address. Lee Erwin left town in the dead of night and later turned up on Arthur Godfrey's show. Jim Runyan threw in the towel and got married—thrice!

It's a frightening sight to see the way Ruth's eyes light up when a happy, carefree bachelor hoves into view. She looks like a hungry tigress that has just spotted a toothsome antelope strolling through the jungle. If you ask me, the antelope was better off than poor Pete at this moment.

This is really the most underhanded trick my fiendish friend has yet to perpetrate. Pete has managed to give the blessed bonds of wedlock a wide berth for well over forty years and he doesn't deserve the fate he is about to meet.

For years, Pete purred romantic poetry into the air waves, via "Moon River," causing the downfall of innocent bachelors all over the country. While his victims were blissfully trapped on porch swings, convertibles and moonlit beaches, Pete has been safely behind a microphone. He has had no problems.

Come to think of it, he is probably getting his comeuppance, but I figure he should be given a fighting chance, at least.

Get out of town, before it's too late, my lad.

And Now a Word from Our Sponsor

_____

There can't be anything wrong with a nation that is wholly dedicated to whiteness—whiter wash, whiter teeth, whiter sinks, etc., not to mention their whiter washing machines!

I can't quite recall when the nation-wide passion came upon us, but it gathers momentum with each passing day. Just recently I was urged to compare my laundry with the enamel on my washing machine. Actually, this particular TV commercial insisted that I MEASURE the whiteness! Now this is a gimmick which should drive the language purists stark staring mad. You can measure flour, floor space or curtains, but how can you measure whiteness?

I am also fascinated by the fact that, on TV, no housewife is ever alone when she does her laundry. Have you noticed that there are always two or more people in a commercial? Never less than two. If it takes two to tango, it also takes two to discuss how to come up with a pristine wash.

Usually you'll find a nosy dame on hand to tell a poor slob what she's doing wrong. I don't know why Mrs. Nosy bothers since the very next day, Mrs. Slob is making the same mistakes.

"Why, Dora, how can you ask a detergent to do a Clorox job?" asks Mrs. Nosy. She's always there to say "I told you so," too.

I must say, Mrs. Nosy gets around to more basements than anyone since good old Charlie, the washing machine repair man. She's so busy minding everyone else's wash that it wonders me how she ever gets her own done.

Mrs. Nosy has another friend named Maisie, who is very short on smart. Maisie keeps hanging up her laundry on a piece of string, which always breaks, landing the clothes on the floor.

"Why, Maisie," says Mrs. Nosy, surveying the mess, "you can't use string for a clothesline!"

I'm afraid she's right, Maisie, but I'll tell you what you can use that string for. . . .

Around her neck, Maisie! Around her neck!

It's hard to say just what ultimate effect TV will have upon the American housefrau, but if we all wind up trailing behind vacuum cleaners in gossamer chiffon negligees, I won't be too astonished.

So far I have managed to resist the temptation to pull my hands out of the dishwater and hold them aloft for general admiration, but it's only because I wear rubber gloves. I imagine, however, most women have a tough time getting the dishes done these days on account of all the time they must spend gazing at their lovely hands.

And if you think the hand bit is time-consuming, think how much trouble it is for a woman to wash her face these days. First she must dress for the project—luckily she can wear the same negligee she cleans house in—and then there is the business of breaking out a new bar of soap. Nobody, but nobody, on TV uses the same bar of soap twice!

There is a special face-washing technique on TV and, having observed thousands of ravishing young ladies wash their faces before the cameras, I feel qualified to pass along some of the basic rules.

First, never wash anywhere near your mouth. This ruins your devastating smile and you're quite likely to get soap in your mouth while telling everyone how clean you feel. And keep the washcloth away from your eyes, too, because they're meant to light up with ecstasy as you're rubbing your petal-like cheeks.

Surely I don't have to remind you NOT to wash your ears. Heaven forfend! Have you ever seen anyone wash her ears on TV? That's worse than wearing last year's mink when you're giving yourself a home permanent!

I must confess I've had a few qualms about TV's bath-taking technique of late and I think I'll just stick to my own archaic method. It may not be accepted in the best circles, but I still think it's more efficient than just washing one arm and one leg, which is all I ever see washed on television. And it's always the same arm and leg, too.

But then, the commercial only lasts for a minute and a half, and what woman was ever born who could take a bath in a minute and a half?

I was certainly shocked the other day when Bob Braun said he wondered if real people talk the way they do in TV commercials. You know, those enlightening little chats about deodorants, laxatives, detergents and headache remedies.

Bob, old buddy, how can you be such a skeptic? Of course, they do. How many times have you come home and said to your wife, Wray Jean: "You look tired, dear. Did you use that weak detergent to wash down the cellar walls again? How many times must I tell you that Nifty Swifty cuts the work in half with a once-over-lightly!"

You just get yourself out from in front of that TV camera, Bob, and find out what real people are talking about these days.

All over town housewives are leaning out of windows telling each other about the glories of new, NEW Snide. When they aren't doing that, they're making like the three monkeys—feeling no grease, seeing no grease and smelling no grease.

Time was when any housewife worthy of the name sat around slurping up coffee in the morning, discussing one neighbor's business with another neighbor.

Not any more.

Any time a koffee klatch gathers these days, the hostess grabs up a pitcher of water to pour over her kitchen floor and prove she uses the right kind of floor wax.

And another thing, Mr. Braun: Don't be loose-lipping my friends Helen and Harry Hart, of the Raleigh cigarette commercials. Everyone who watches TV knows that Helen and Harry Hart have furnished at least four houses with cigarette coupons. They have both quit their jobs to devote their full time to chain-smoking on a twenty-four-hour-a-day basis.

The last time I dropped in on Helen and Harry Hart, I had trouble getting into their house. They had parked their new Chris Craft cruiser in the living room and I had to climb in a window.

As always, the room was so blue with smoke I could barely see Helen and Harry but I finally found them where the smoke was thickest.

"Look," chortled Harry, lighting one cigarette from the end of another, "I've taught Helen to smoke three cigarettes at once—one in each ear. Next month, they're giving us Fort Knox."

As another of my many services on behalf of my readers, I've been keeping score on which rooms in the American home appear most frequently in TV commercials.

It may interest you to know, friends, that the bathroom is rapidly outstripping both the kitchen and the laundry as a setting for the ladies and gentlemen who pitch the products.

I've grown accustomed to the sight of countless glamor girls washing cheeks, chin and forehead—but almost never their noses. I have lost track of the number of people who have taken baths and showers on my TV set, or those who brush their teeth and gargle so enthusiastically. But, just recently, a new member of the Bathroom Brigade has joined this cast of thousands. He dances!

The star of this enchanting true-life drama, Our Hero, has just emerged joyfully from the shower, grabbing up a Fiesta towel. He is overcome by the beauty of the towel—prior to that, I assume, he just let the air dry him—and, suddenly, a full orchestra (concealed in the linen closet, no doubt) busts loose with foot-stomping, finger-snapping Spanish music.

Between the sheer ecstasy of finally having a towel, and of hearing an orchestra in the linen closet, Our Hero is completely carried away and immediately goes into a spirited flamenco dance, beating his feet on the floor and snapping the fingers of one hand. He can only snap the fingers of one hand because it is vital that he clutch the towel with the other hand. Television has not progressed THAT far.

Unfortunately, the commercial is too brief to allow time for what surely must be the ending of this fascinating slice of life. Our Hero's wife, hearing all the activity in the bathroom—foot-stomping, finger-snapping and that band going full blast—starts to hammer on the bathroom door.

"For heaven's sake, Harry, what's going on in there?" she hollers.

"What do you think is going on in here?" Harry hollers back. "I'm stomping out ants!"

Sometimes, as I watch my TV screen get sticky with those gooey glimpses of Mrs. Olsen saving another rocky marriage with a pound of Folger's coffee, I wonder what happened to that "loaf of bread, a jug of wine and thou beside me" image of romance? Has an entire nation of lovers succumbed to a pot of coffee?

And what of Mrs. Olsen's love life? Is there a Mr. Olsen waiting in the wings as our Swedish Ann Landers flits from kitchen to kitchen lugging her copious reticule filled with cans of Folger's coffee?

Or has Mr. Olsen, awash with coffee and finally unable to lift a cup in his trembling hands, gone back to the old country where he now steadies his coffee nerves with gallons of Aquavit?

A relentless Cupid, almost nobody is safe from Mrs. Olsen these days. When she isn't saving marriages, she is busy herding young couples into wedlock with the clear intention of having more marital problems to solve in the future.

It's spring, Mrs. Olsen, the season of champagne. Try toting some of that around in your reticule and I'm willing to bet you'll be welcome in a lot more kitchens. You might even get into a bedroom from time to time.

Often, as I see the endless parade of Mrs. Olsens, Katy Winters, the Queen of Deodorant pitchwomen, and little tots lisping paeans of praise to laundry starch, I wonder: Did God really intend for pictures to fly through the air?

As I sit of an evening, elegantly attired in bluejeans and a beat-up sweat shirt, I am plunged headlong into a world of gracious living through the courtesy of the FM radio commercials.

Quite often, as I listen enthralled, I feel compelled to slip into black lace and pearls as the announcers extol the ecstasy of sipping rare wines and dining—by candlelight, of course—on exquisite cuisine.

"Why aren't you sipping champagne?" I ask myself, staring gloomily into my martini. "With such an inspiring message ringing in your ears, it ain't fittin' you should be sitting here drinking gin!"

One is treated with such finesse by those FM announcers. I am enchanted—nay, flattered—by their unshakable assumption that I am the kind of person whose elegance would be enhanced by driving a pre-owned Cadillac. The former owner of the Caddy, it goes without saying, was a bank president who was unable to keep up the payments. Naturally, on FM radio, one does not stoop to such crass terms as "used" or "second-hand" cars. Perish forbid!

In pear-shaped tones, my unseen advisers assure me that I am a woman of taste and discrimination, whose wardrobe would include only girdles of sheerest mink because of my dedicated attention to the smallest detail. One shudders to consider what might happen if one sullied the seat of a pre-owned Cadillac with a garment unworthy of The Real Me.

There is no end to the services performed by FM radio. I wait with bated breath for the heady moment when I am given the latest word from Wall Street. Is General Motors off a point? Will U. S. Steel hold steady? Thank God AT&T had a good day!

And how comforting to know that whether one is in Paris or Caracas, one's trusted investment counselor will review one's holdings. It will be his pleasure.

It would be mine, too, if I had any to review.

Elgiva Flye phoned from Dismal Seepage yesterday with some pretty exciting news about her husband, Horst Flye.

"I tell you, Mary, Dismal Seepage is all atwitter," bubbled Elgiva. "Horst is writing an opera!"

"You're putting me on," I said.

"No, it's true," she insisted, "and you'll never believe where he got the idea."

Knowing Horst, I realized that any time he gets an idea—no matter from where—it's news.

"The other night, when that Bold commercial came on —you know the one; where the two housewives duet in that beautiful aria, 'Pinkier Pinks, Whitier Whites, and Stripier Stripes'?" Elgiva went on, "Horst said to me, 'Elgiva,' he said, 'I think I'll just write me an opera.' You could have knocked me over with a feather-light Duncan Hines cake."

The characters in Horst's opera, which he has tentatively titled *The Madison Avenue Story*, will be drawn from the people he knows and loves in TV commercials, Elgiva explained.

"In the opening scene, the Knight on the white horse

rescues Mrs. Olsen from a mob gone berserk from coffee nerves," she said.

"Later, there is a pitched battle between the Jolly Green Giant and the Giant in the washing machine, accompanied by a swelling chorus of 'Things Go Better With Coke' sung by a group of the Jolly Green Giant's elves."

"You haven't told me whether the opera is tragedy or comedy," I mentioned. "How does it wind up?"

"It's a tragedy, of course," said Elgiva. "Our heroine is a modern housewife, ever anxious to provide her family with the better things in life. She squeezes the Charmin, dunks roses in her dishwater, smashes Alka-Seltzer tablets, washes her baby's burlap diapers in special softeners and spends hours discussing detergents with her friends. At the end of the opera, she cracks up."

"How come?" I asked. "She seems like a perfectly normal American housewife to me."

"Believe me, Mary, there won't be a dry eye during the last scene—The Mad Scene. It's the finest moment in the opera," said Elgiva.

"What happens?" I asked breathlessly.

"Her deodorant soap fails her!" sobbed Elgiva.

I may finally be forced to give up smoking. It's not that I'm worried about my health, it's just that a feeling of inadequacy and inferiority plagues me when I watch cigarette commercials on TV.

I'm not tattooed. I've never launched a rocket ship into outer space. They said it couldn't be done and they were right. I couldn't do it.

I'm reasonably sure I could never smoke a cigarette while sailing along on water skis, but lowest of all blows to my withered ego is the intellectual snob approach— The Thinking Man! He smokes the right cigarette because he reads Christopher Marlowe's *Dr. Faustus*. Or maybe it's the other way around.

I've never read *Dr. Faustus*. I tried once, but I probably wasn't smoking the right cigarette. I couldn't get through it.

It's the class distinction that is getting me down. Gone is the day when a body could buy a pack of cigarettes and just smoke them. Now a body must give pause for deep reflection. Is this cigarette really ME? Am I truly the type of person who should be allowed to smoke this cigarette? Will I be accepted into the inner circle of the intelligentsia? Will I be loved by The Jet Set? Will I be accepted by the crème de la crème of the sports world? Or will I be revealed as a fraud? An imposter, smoking under false colors?

This painful dilemma has been creeping up on me for months, but it burst into full flower the other night, plunging me into the depths of gloom.

There I sat watching TV, clad in my beat-up bluejeans and scratching the ears of my unpedigreed dog, when I was favored with a glimpse of a distinguished member of the upper classes, impeccably attired, reading what certainly must have been a first edition of *Dr. Faustus* in his classy, pine-paneled library.

During the brief, but impressive interview which ensued, I was assured that this was a Thinking Man who had chosen a Smoking Man's filter.

I was thinking, too. I was thinking, whatever became of those nice, comfortable Bull Durham ads? They didn't seem to give a hoot what sort of slobs bought that tobacco as long as they could pay for it!

"The Health of My Burro Is Good"

I am back from Mexico with a somewhat firmer grasp on the Spanish language than I had when I departed, mumbling my only two words—*sí* and *gracias*. But there is one slight hitch. What I can say in Spanish isn't likely to arise in any conversation I'll ever encounter in this world or the next.

Who, I ask you, is about to be fascinated by the information that "Neither my father nor my mother knows that I am no longer attending school?"

For this and other equally enlightening phrases, such as "The house, the orchards and the crops all disappeared with the flood," I am indebted to a column entitled "How's Your Spanish?" which appears in the Mexico City *Daily Bulletin*. Thanks to "How's Your Spanish?" I left a number of Mexicans not only badly shaken, but convinced that their immigration laws should be tightened immediately.

I still remember the look of wonder and astonishment on the face of the cab driver on whom I rehearsed "Rich and poor, beggars and thieves, no one can escape pain." Due to my faulty pronunciation of this inspiring message, he was under the impression that I was calling him a beggar and a thief. We parted almost immediately and not the best of friends, I might add.

As you can see, the editor of "How's Your Spanish?" has a tendency to look upon the gloomy side of life and his students aren't spreading any conversational sunshine around Mexico, either, with such stuff as: "My father (or mother) is starving. He (or she) will soon die."

Follow that up with this cheery gambit: "We will attend the funeral and mourn together," and you're sure to be a success at any social gathering South of the Border.

During the entire period of my close association with "How's Your Spanish?" I only managed to learn one optimistic sentence with which to enhance my conversation. Unfortunately, since my mode of transportation differed from the subject of the sentence, I was never able to use it, but here it is in case you ever need it:

"The health of my burro is good."

LONDON . . . You can mention my name to the Lord Mayor of Nottingham, friends, but please don't tell him where I am. He's trying to forget and so am I. They tell me that in one afternoon I managed to set British protocol back one hundred years.

And all the time I was under the impression I was exuding charm and graciousness upon the Lord Mayor, on whose right I had been seated, and the Lord High Sheriff, who managed to escape me by three seats.

We American columnists were transported to Nottingham—some hundred and twenty miles from London—to be entertained by the Lord Mayor at an official banquet. This was my first mistake. I was under the impression it was simply an informal luncheon.

I suppose I should have gotten a slight hint from the impressive fellow in tails who busted up the pre-luncheon cocktail session by pounding a gavel and announcing in stentorian tones: "Pray Silence, luncheon is served."

I'll admit I was impressed but not to the point of being deterred from being the first at the table and the first seated. I wondered why everyone was standing around until Tails-and-Gavel pounded his gavel again and issued this order: "Pray Silence. You have the Lord Mayor's permission to be seated."

It took a moment or two for me to put on my shoes again and stand up with the rest of the company. By then, they were seated and I was up.

Well, the Lord Mayor and I bobbed around a couple of times and finally went down together.

At this point, I was pretty well shaken up so I offered the Lord Mayor a cigarette—which he refused—and lit one myself. I had just about finished the cigarette when Tails-and-Gavel beat a rousing tattoo on the gavel again and cried: "Pray Silence. You have the Lord Mayor's permission to smoke."

About this time the waiters came around with the wine, which I managed to dispose of in one gulp, there being no water in sight.

So I am staring at my empty glass when old Tails-and-Gavel went to work again with: "Pray Silence. The Lord Mayor will now propose a toast to the Queen and the President of the United States!"

And there I sat with an empty glass!

By now, as you can well imagine, I had come utterly unglued. It then fell to me to present the Lord High Sheriff and his Lady with a pewter goblet as a token of the columnists' joint esteem. I did have enough foresight to scribble down the correct titles but, unfortunately, the waiter had somehow made off with my notes so I was forced to ad lib. They tell me it came out like this: "Your Holiness Lord and Lady Sheriff!"

Well, I tried.

Your Ancient Mariner is home from sailing the Caribbean, dragging her albatross behind her!

As I departed the comfort and joyous company at my favorite inn on St. Thomas—Gramboko—my friend and landlady, Ellie Heckert said: "Any middle-aged dame who takes off on a sailboat for twelve days has got to be out of her mind!"

Never were truer, more prophetic words spoken. There are people at rest in Spring Grove Cemetery in far better shape than I.

The voyage of your Ancient Mariner to the Windward Islands, aboard the *Yankee Clipper*, got off to an auspicious beginning when I stepped off the dock in St. Maarten and into the Caribbean Ocean, fully clothed and clutching my straw bag which contained such vital equipment as money, traveler's checks and airline ticket home. I bobbed up like a cork, bruised, battered and full of sea urchin needles, but still clutching straw bag full of wet money, traveler's checks and airline ticket home, and was hauled aboard the *Clipper*.

Now if I'd had a brain in my head, I would have dried out my ticket and caught the next plane home—

but no. Off I go, over the bounding main, with every bone in my body aching.

I take that back. Since I had managed NOT to hit my left arm, it didn't hurt. But that didn't last long. The first day out, on rough seas, a large wave hit the *Clipper*, causing the ship to lurch violently and me to make a non-stop flight from one side of the salon to the other, landing on my left side. Now every square inch of me hurt evenly and my disposition was somewhat similar to that of an enraged cobra.

I might point out that nothing is easy on a sailboat cruising over the bounding main. Even trying to drink a cup of coffee could be likened to attempting to carry a full bedpan on horseback. The safest way to get from place to place on deck is to crawl on all fours, where you will undoubtedly be as uncomfortable as you were the last place you were on deck.

On the ninth day out, just as my purple bruises were beginning to blend with my expensive tan, I caught a cold—the only cold in the Caribbean.

"What do you have for your cold?" inquired nice Dr. Morter, from Milwaukee.

"Kleenex," I replied dismally. So he gave me some pills and I took to my bunk, where the mattress was stuffed with solid concrete.

The last night out, when I could see the lights of St. Maarten looming ahead, I was sitting on the foredeck congratulating myself on still being alive. The moon was glorious, the sea was calm and I had, so far, escaped burial at sea.

At that moment, right under my nose, the assistant cook pulled out a knife and stabbed the head cook!

Fortunately, the wounds weren't too serious and Dr. Morter, not having envisioned being called upon to sew up the chief cook while vacationing, was able to paste him together with adhesive tape.

Nerves shattered, nose running and bruised from head to foot, I finally arrived at Pasanggrahan, one of the loveliest small guest houses on St. Maarten, where the manager is a friend, Scout Thirkell.

"How did you enjoy your sail?" asked Scout.

"Scout," I replied, "if ever you see me step foot on a sailboat again, I only hope you'll have me committed."

I made a shattering discovery while vacationing on St. Thomas, in the Virgin Islands. My favorite landlady, Ellie Heckert, of Gramboko Inn, introduced me to three submarine officers and, in the course of our conversation, I found that there is a wide gap between the *Seaview*, the sub on "Voyage to the Bottom of the Sea," and the submarines which cause our enemies to tremble.

"Tell me," I asked Commander Denver McCune, "how do you fellows handle the sea monsters you run into?"

"That's something we're working on," replied Commander McCune. "Actually, at the moment the Navy has no procedure for sea monsters, but we have two admirals who do nothing but watch 'Voyage to the Bottom of the Sea' and we expect to come up with a firm plan before the season is over."

Commander Bill Smith, skipper of the USS *Cavalla*, said that he had been deeply concerned about his sub being swallowed by a monster whale until he had observed how the matter was handled by Commander Crane (David Hedison) and Admiral Nelson (Richard Basehart).

"The thing to do is keep a level head and not panic," explained Skipper Smith. "It's well to remember that

state department have been very understanding."

This is Terry's first job as a superintendent. He has been working in education for 19 years, he said. About half of that time has been spent at high schools and the other half at colleges. His most recent job was a coaching/teaching position at Carthage High School.

"I saw this as an opportunity to get into administration," he said of the job opening at Grady. "I've

"I know from experience, that you don't reach these children the primary level, they are hard reach," she said. "What can we to reach them?"

Ms. Jasper voiced not only

many members of your crew may never have seen the inside of a whale's belly before and will look upon being there as a jolly lark.

"My plan would be to give the men a day's liberty so they could get out of the sub and poke around, and then give the whale an enormous dose of ipecac which would cause it to regurgitate the ship," he continued. "We carry several hundred gallons of ipecac for just such an emergency."

The officers assured me that watching "Voyage" had been invaluable to them in their work, especially since the *Seaview* was the only sub they had ever known which had the full-time services of an admiral. It is also the only sub which sends divers out at three-hundred-foot depth.

"Our boys won't go," said Lieutenant Commander Demo Kolaras. "They chicken out at two hundred feet."

Commander Smith hoped wistfully to get a sub with a big picture window and a wardroom the size of a ballroom for his next command but, so far, the Navy has not seen fit to build any sub quite as lavish as the *Seaview.*

"But at least we don't get a lot of mad scientists with beautiful daughters aboard our ships," he said. "Having a mad scientist aboard can be troublesome and the Navy has never issued us any instructions on how to handle them."

"Hell, they've never told us how to handle the beautiful daughters, either," Commander McCune pointed out, "but it's like facing up to any other unpleasant duty. You assign it to the executive officer."

I've been to Washington to look at the queen of party-givers, the hostess with the mostess, Mrs. Perle Mesta. My rather hectic debut in Washington society came about when I attended a gala reception given by Mrs. Mesta.

Arriving in Washington at high noon, I repaired at once in quest of my friend Wauhillau LaHay, of Scripps-Howard News, who is called "Wauhillha" by Lady Bird Johnson.

"Honey," I said, because I can't pronounce her name, "all my constituents back in Cincinnati and several adjoining Kentucky counties are expecting me to do them proud at this party. What would you suggest?"

"Well, I would suggest that they had sent somebody else," she replied, "but apparently it's too late now. What had you planned to wear?"

"I plan to be a vision of loveliness in my daughter Sally's red chiffon dinner dress," I said, with some hostility. "This is my banner year, fashion-wise. Sally is having another baby and I am helping her by wearing all her clothes. I am, however, wearing my own underwear and shoes. She can still wear her shoes, I'm sorry to say."

"I'll see you at the party," sighed Wauhillau. "Smile a lot."

Wreathed in smiles and red chiffon, I arrived at Mrs. Mesta's penthouse apartment—fifteen rooms, if you care to count. Mrs. Mesta greeted me warmly and I beamed upon Mrs. Mesta. I not only beamed, I was darn near blinded by her diamond necklace which fairly paved her neck. At once, I knew I was wearing the wrong jewelry.

About that time Wauhillau whipped by, hissing that His Excellency, The Irish Ambassador, was in the offing and was willing to meet me if I would just stand still. Since His Excellency and I had about as much chance of NOT meeting as a couple of sardines in a can, we met. I also met his wife, a charming lady, who was caught in the same sardine can.

"I'm delighted to meet you, Your Mrs. Excellency," I shouted in her ear. "Sorry to hear of your trouble."

"Yes," she shouted back, "they're all well."

At this point the butler announced the arrival of Mr. and Mrs. Ray Bliss, a familiar name though we had never met.

Oozing away from Her Mrs. Excellency, I forged through Mrs. Mesta's three hundred most intimate friends toward Mr. and Mrs. Bliss. By now it was every dame for herself and the red chiffon was getting rather rumpled. I didn't figure to be a vision of loveliness much longer.

Wauhillau would have been overcome with pride at my performance in greeting Mr. and Mrs. Bliss—up to a point. As I fought my way valiantly through Mrs. Gwen Cafritz, Jackie Cooper, the Ambassador of Iran and assorted waiters bearing trays of pink champagne, I finally cornered Mr. and Mrs. Bliss hanging over a plate of goodies.

"How are you?" I asked, with great warmth and a winning smile. "I am from Ohio."

"That's nice," said Mr. Bliss.

"Well, really, I'm not from Ohio," I said, trying to be friendly, but honest. "I live in Kentucky."

"That's nice," said Mr. Bliss, confused but still game.

"I thought you were a Republican," I said—why I shall never know except that Wauhillau had said it was vital to keep talking because, at these parties, nobody ever hears what you say, anyway. Unfortunately, Mr. Bliss heard me—loud and clear.

"I am a Republican," he replied firmly. "I'd like for you to meet my wife. She's a Republican, too."

In departing the gala affair, after I had made my manners to Mrs. Mesta, I had the feeling that Washington society had lost a great potential in me. But the Iron Butterfly can only spread her wings so far.

"Come Spend a Quiet Weekend with Us, Mama"

It happens every June to thousands of mothers. The organist plays "Here Comes the Bride" and you look up to see a radiant young stranger, clad in a white wedding gown and holding a bouquet, walking slowly down the aisle.

"Now where have I seen this girl before?" you ask yourself and, suddenly, it all comes back to you.

This was that red, wrinkled, squalling bundle of humanity the nurse brought into your hospital room twenty-one years ago and said: "Isn't she lovely?"

"What is it?" you asked groggily.

"It's your daughter," she said.

It was an introduction that began a long and close relationship, closer than you'll ever have with anyone else. Happy, sad, loving, hostile, tender, wrathful, frustrating, fulfilling—but never dull.

How did either of you manage to survive that first bath you gave her? Or those 2 A.M. bottles when you first learned to walk in your sleep?

Remember that first beatific smile she gave you which her pediatrician assured you was not affection—just gas?

Will you ever forget that harried morning when she

slipped out of her play pen and toddled stark naked to the grocery three blocks away to get a cookie?

And the wonderful discoveries you made together— like Winnie, the Pooh—when you found that little children have a delightfully fey sense of humor?

That long, heart-breaking night when her fever climbed to 106 and you sat beside her helpless and frightened . . . the stomach-aches and broken arm?

There was her first letter to you from summer camp: "Dear Mama, I miss you and Captain Video. A horse stepped on my face."

Then, almost before you realized it could happen, she lost interest in collecting dolls and began collecting boys. You knew this had happened when she demanded high heels and you watched her totter off to her first dance, hoping she wouldn't sprain an ankle going down the front steps on the arm of that high school freshman you hardly recognized out of his bluejeans.

The battles you've had . . . "I'll give you just five minutes to make your bed, young lady!" . . . and the laughs . . . "I'll be glad to teach you the Charleston, but when they bring back the minuet, I don't know it."

The day she went off to college accompanied by most of your stockings and slips and your two best sweaters.

The night she woke you at 2 A.M. to show you her engagement ring and you talked until dawn.

And now her happy day is here and there she stands at the altar exchanging marriage vows with a tall, handsome boy you met four years ago, never dreaming he'd turn out to be your son-in-law.

You know that this is the beginning of a new life for her and you're grateful for having been a part of the old one.

You also know that the most wonderful experience anyone can ever have is rearing a daughter.

An old verse comes back to you—a sort of silent fare-
well:

> I turn from you and try to smile,
> But tears, like clouds of stinging insects,
> Bite my lids.

This horrendous saga will serve as a warning to those of you who are grandmothers and others who someday may be.

I spent last week at Topsail Beach, North Carolina, with my daughter and son-in-law, Sally and Sandy Thomson. They have two babies, Dougie, age two, and Betsy, who is six months old. Also visiting were Nancy and Don Gurney, with fourteen-month-old Scottie.

Get the picture? Five adults and three darling, adorable and extremely active children.

So one morning the parents of these three darling, adorable and extremely active children set out to go deep-sea fishing.

"Don't worry about a thing, Mama," said Sally. "We want you to rest and relax, so we've hired a baby-sitter for the day. The baby-sitter will be here at 8 A.M. and all you have to do is give the kids breakfast and change their diapers until she gets here. Nancy and I will leave you a list of instructions."

Promptly at 5 A.M. the happy fisherfolk departed, first shaking me out of a sound slumber.

"The kids are all awake but I don't think the hostilities will break out before six o'clock," beamed Nancy.

She couldn't have been more wrong. The first scream of anguish came at 5:30 A.M. and was soon joined by two more.

Leaping from bed, I grabbed the list of instructions. "Change diapers" headed the list. While all three bellowed at the top of their darling, adorable and extremely strong lungs, I launched on the diaper-changing project.

May I digress for a moment to tell you about modern diaper pins? They're a far cry from the safety pins I remember. Nowadays, diaper pins are tricked out with cute heads of bunnies, bears and pussy cats. You need a degree in mechanical engineering to get one of the blasted things open or shut.

Meanwhile, back to the diaper project . . . as fast as I got one kid dry, the other two were wet again.

"Be with you in a minute," I yelled frantically. That was silly since all three were yelling so loud they couldn't hear me anyway.

Breakfast time was set, according to instructions, at 7 A.M., with Betsy first on the list. I started her breakfast of cereal and strained fruit at 6:30 in the faint and foolish hope that a baby with a mouthful of food can't holler.

How can one small child get so much cereal and strained fruit in her hair, eyes, ears and so little in her mouth?

By the time Betsy's breakfast was over, all three were wet again. One was screaming for Mommie and the other for "kookie." I gave both vanilla wafers and shuddered to think what my late and great pediatrician, Dr. Horace Stewart, would have done to me.

Having triumphantly achieved getting all three dry at

once, I attempted to put the older two into high chairs. Have you ever tried to place a squirming, reluctant child in a high chair?

By now, I was talking to myself to keep up my spirits.

"Give Betsy her bottle and make toast for the boys," I muttered. "Then cut your throat."

What my darling daughter had neglected to tell me was that putting toast in her toaster does not guarantee that it will pop up with toast. It catches fire.

So, suddenly, as I was giving Betsy her bottle, the kitchen was filled with billows of smoke.

At that point, the baby-sitter walked in the door. For once the kids, fascinated by the smoke, were quiet. I was crying!

"Anything happen?" asked the baby-sitter.

"Come and spend a nice, quiet weekend with us, Mama," urged my daughter Sally. She and her husband, Sandy Thomson, had just moved from Oxford, Ohio, to Columbus.

So I went, and I want all you fellow grandmothers to know that there is nothing like a nice quiet weekend in the bosom of your family to take ten years off your life.

Sally and Sandy looked haggard and hollow-eyed when I drove up. Not their children, Dougie, age four, and Betsy, who is two and a half. They were, as always, in fine fettle.

"Mandy had six pookers last night, Nini," Dougie announced. "They are black pookers and I am their brother."

"Pookers?" I asked. "He must mean puppies."

"He means pookers," said Sally grimly. "Mandy's a cocker spaniel and these pookers are the result of a warm friendship with a black poodle in Oxford, the cad.

"Sandy and I were up until 5:30 A.M.," she added. "Never again."

Dougie, his arms loaded with picture books, retired to the basement to entertain the pookers.

"He's been showing them pictures of dogs and telling

them about Lassie all morning," Sally explained. "Now if you'll read *Peter Rabbit* to Betsy, I'll go take a nap."

I have the rare distinction of being the leading reader of *Peter Rabbit* in the Thomson clan.

"Flopsy, Mopsy and Cottontail are good wittle wabbits," Betsy assured me. "They mind their Mama. Peter is a naughty wittle wabbit."

"You better believe it," said I, preparing to dispose of that no-goodnik Peter in short order.

I am never quite prepared for the crises which seem to arise each time I visit Sally and Sandy, but I'm becoming more adjusted as time goes on. The next morning, at the bust of dawn, I was jolted out of dreamland by Sally, standing over my bed, weeping copiously.

"Get up, Mama," she sobbed. "Mandy is very sick and Sandy and I are rushing her to the vet. We think she has another puppy she didn't deliver. Betsy is fixing breakfast."

"Betsy is WHAT?" I howled, leaping out of the feathers.

"That's what she says she's doing," replied her mother. "We'll see you later. Don't worry."

There's a two-and-a-half-year-old child in the kitchen fixing breakfast and I shouldn't worry! Several track records were broken during my dash to the kitchen.

"I am helping you," beamed Betsy, licking the sugar off a large caramel bun. "I am putting wolls in the oven."

Several "wolls," licked sugarless, graced the oven. A great deal of sugar graced Betsy's face.

"Dougie is naughty like Peter Wabbit," Betsy reported. "He took off all his clothes."

"Good grief, where is he?" I asked wildly.

"He went to play with his friends," Betsy replied calmly.

More track records were broken in quest of Dougie. He was discovered, still wearing his underpants, reading to the pookers again. The pookers were not happy without their Mama and quite vocal about it.

Sally phoned from the vet's to say all was well with Mandy.

"Why don't you stay for dinner, Mama, and we'll have a nice, quiet visit," she suggested.

Sooner or later, into the life of every grandmother, comes a trip to the Zoo, complete with picnic lunch, very small grandchildren and a tour of the Monkey House.

Yes, grandmothers, that multicolored baboon you recall so vividly is still there.

Dougie Thomson and his sister Betsy set out with Nini Wood (that's what they call me) in my Volkswagen.

"Why is your car so little?" inquired Dougie, who recently discovered that the magic word is "why."

"Because it hasn't grown up yet," I replied, congratulating myself on having come up with at least one answer so early in the game.

"Why?" countered Dougie.

"Ask your sister," I parried.

On arriving at the Zoo, we immediately boarded a small train. I figured this might well be my last opportunity to sit down for several hours.

"Why are you holding Betsy?" asked her brother.

"So she won't fall off the train," I explained.

"Betsy wants to fall off the train," he announced confidently. "Then the bears will eat her up."

I shuddered and took a firmer grip on Betsy.

The Children's Zoo was a howling success except that

Dougie insisted that we take the three little pigs home with us. Betsy fell madly in love with a white rabbit which she was loathe to relinquish. There was a traumatic moment for Nini at the sea lion tank when they both decided to join the sea lions.

Becoming increasingly conscious of my feet, I suggested we all sit down and eat lunch. Dougie surveyed the sandwiches and deviled eggs with something less than enthusiasm.

"I want chicken noodle soup," he said.

"Betsy likes sandwiches," I pointed out. "She's eating her sandwich."

"The bears will eat up Betsy," Dougie announced darkly. "The bears will eat you up, too."

The moment had come, I felt, to quell the dissension with ice cream cones. Unfortunately, time had dimmed my memory concerning the tendency of ice cream cones to melt rapidly in the hot sun. Betsy, who is happiest when her mouth is full, did her best to keep abreast of the melting cone, but it was a losing battle. Within minutes, she was stem to stern ice cream. I didn't know there was so much ice cream in the world!

"Betsy's messy," said her loving brother, delivering the understatement of the week.

Having reclaimed as much of Betsy as possible with the aid of wet paper napkins, our happy little band set off for the Monkey House. Too late I remembered that blasted baboon, but there he was with his brilliant, eye-catching cerise behind. He was also still up to his old tricks I sharply recalled from the days when my daughter Sally was five years old and we visited the Zoo. I could almost predict Dougie's next question because I'd heard it before.

"Look at the funny monkey, Nini," shrilled Dougie. "What's he doing?"

Looking back on Christmas Day, which I spent with the young Thomson Clan in Columbus, I can't recall a more memorable day. It began at the break of dawn when Miss Betsy Thomson, clad only in her Mouseketeer cap, rose to sing her version of "Silent Night."

"Silent night, early night," caroled Betsy cheerfully. "Holy elephant so tender and wild!"

In record time the living room was reduced to shambles. All seven dolls had their shoes and socks removed, a bloody battle was in progress at the Frontier Fort between the Indians and the Bluecoats and the roar of Dougie's Vvv-rooooom Big Job dump truck precluded any exchange of Christmas greetings.

Some day I hope to meet the fiend who invented Vvv-rooooom Big Job! In my opinion, this man is a menace to all adults and should be dealt with accordingly, preferably put in the same room with one of his Vvv-rooooom Big Job's going full-blast.

A heated argument arose concerning the Frontier Fort since both Betsy and Dougie wanted to be the Indians, and no one was willing to be Bluecoats. Finally, my son-in-law Sandy, a former Marine, volunteered to be the Bluecoats and was badly beaten in the fray.

Somewhat bruised by frequent encounters with the doll buggy, which kept flying by, I suggested that Betsy gather all seven dolls, complete with assorted shoes and socks, into the buggy and take them for a long ride in the kitchen. A frantic search for the shoes and socks ensued, one being found in my drink.

"Now we will have a birthday party for the doll babies and sing 'Little Lord Jesus,'" Betsy announced, "but one doll baby can't come."

"Why not?" I asked.

"Because she has the measles, the mumps and poison ivy," Betsy explained.

No grandmother should count herself a member of the club until she has visited the Zoo and Coney Island accompanied by at least two grandchildren. Any less and she's chickened out. Last year, I made the Zoo single-handed. This year, with my wits about me, I conned my fellow grandmother, Adele Thomson, and my daughter Sally into a Sunday afternoon at Coney Island with Miss Betsy Thomson, age three and a half, and her brother Dougie, who has lately achieved his fifth year.

With Sally bringing up the rear, acting as though she hardly knew us, Adele and I clutched a grandchild each, bravely forging ahead to The Land of Oz. We were temporarily waylaid en route by the merry-go-round for which I have great sentimental attachment. It happens to be the only ride on which I have never gotten violently sick.

Reeling slightly from two trips on the merry-go-round, our joyful band arrived at the Land of Oz and the Jolly Caterpillar. Betsy, the family daredevil, found this far more exciting than the up-and-down horses, but it was pale beside the Teddy Bear for whetting her appetite for living dangerously.

Since the Teddy Bear is the first roller coaster I've ever really been happy on, I was reluctant to leave it,

particularly when Betsy announced that the Wild Mouse
was more her speed. We departed only because Dougie
had inside information that a bloody Indian massacre
was in progress on the other side of the park which could
be observed, in perfect safety, from a train. We boarded
the train, dodging Indian arrows and settlers' bullets.
A most exciting trip.

"Why doesn't Nini Wood have Indians at her house,"
Betsy inquired of her mother.

"She does but they're away on vacation," explained
her mother, not wanting to destroy Nini Wood's image.

Betsy was greatly taken with the timber wolf in the
wilds of Coney's Frontier, but Nini Thomson discouraged
taking the wolf on the Swiss Sky Ride, which was our
next adventure. Even without Betsy's timber wolf, the
Swiss Sky Ride could be counted as eminently successful.
Dougie said he planned to spend the rest of his life on
it, but we were running low on tickets.

It was decided that Betsy wasn't quite ready for the
Lost River—"Next year, Betsy, next year"—but her grief
was somewhat assuaged by the assurance that Nini
Thomson and her mother could hardly wait to hear her
sing the entire score of *Mary Poppins*. Betsy, we have
great hope, will be the next Bobby Breen.

At any rate, Dougie and I embarked on the Lost River
alone, except for an amorous young couple in the seat
ahead, locked in tender embrace.

"Why is he kissing her?" asked Dougie, at the top of
his lungs.

"Because they're friends," I explained frantically.

"Mark is my friend, but I don't kiss him," said Dougie.
"Do you like Mark?"

Since we were getting some black looks from Amorous Couple, I was only too glad to talk about Mark—and anybody else.

"Sure I like Mark," I said, vaguely recalling a small boy who resembled a sheep dog.

"Mark says bad words," said Dougie darkly.

"Like what?" I asked, prepared for the worst.

"He says potty," announced Dougie. "Now do you like him?"

I can only say that, with Dougie as his friend, Mark will never be in need of an enemy!

I have finally achieved the ultimate success as a grand-mother. I took my grandson, Dougie Thomson, to visit Uncle Al Lewis' show. To Dougie, Uncle Al and Captain Windy are all the Beatles rolled into two—if you happen to be a teen-ager, which Dougie isn't. But the ecstasy is the same. Dougie's eyes were twice their normal size for an hour and a half.

Driving to the studio, Dougie and I discussed a burning question: Could Captain Windy really fly? I remarked that there was a possibility that she might not fly every day.

"She flied yesterday," said Dougie flatly, "so she'll fly today."

There were twenty-five sets of twins visiting Uncle Al when we arrived—the cutest aggregation of The Sticky Finger Set I've yet to see. We were a few minutes late and the show was going strong when we arrived. Uncle Al's straw hat could be barely distinguished in the midst of a sea of small, bobbing heads, but his accordion was coming through loud and clear. From that moment on, there wasn't a dull split second.

In all the years I've watched Uncle Al on TV, that was the first time I'd visited his show. May I say that it is a minor miracle of timing, production and organization. Something is going on every moment to amuse the youngsters, who are made to feel a part of the program. Al and Wanda make every effort to put the spotlight on the children and make them feel important.

WLW Radio's Bill Myers was represented by his twin daughters, Kathleen and Michele, who favored us with two songs from *Mary Poppins*. They're utterly adorable five-year-olds and not a bit camera-shy.

Mama Marianne explained: "They take after their father—hammy!"

Dougie's cup of happiness was filled to the brim when he was chosen to be the Traffic Cop in the auto race. He gladly kissed the winner—a little girl—which was another triumph for Uncle Al. At this point, Dougie takes a dim view of kissing girls unless they happen to be a lot older than five and then only under duress. Mothers and grandmothers, Dougie has found, are kissing fools.

"Captain Windy really does fly," Dougie told me as we floated home on Cloud Nine.

"You bet she does," I replied. "It's the only way to get in and out of Dagwood's bathroom every day."

Miss Betsy Thomson, who is four and a half, and her brother Dougie, who is six, spent last weekend with Nini Wood. Now that Nini Wood has gotten the remnants of the peanut butter and jelly out of her hair, the crayons and jacks (have you ever stepped on a jack in your bare feet?) up off the carpet and taken a tranquilizer, she will attempt to reconstruct the events of our two fun-filled days.

First, may I say that the greatest boon to grandmothers ever devised is those early-morning cartoon shows on TV. I was on my knees both mornings offering up a fervent prayer of thanksgiving for those cartoons.

Having paid our respects to all the dogs on Riverside Drive, and the next-door neighbor's cat, our happy group set out for Coney Island at high noon on Saturday. The Batcave was our first stop and Betsy kept her eyes tightly shut during our tour in order NOT to see the scary spiders. However, Dougie obliged with such a lurid description of the monsters he had beheld in the Batcave that she insisted on going again—this time with her eyes open.

"If Betsy fell out," remarked Dougie, as we soared

over Coney in the Swiss Sky Ride, "she would be all mashed up on the ground."

I agreed and took a firmer grip on Betsy.

Since my daughter Sally had assured me that it was impossible for two healthy children to die of malnutrition in two days, I took the easy way and fed them anything they wanted. What they wanted was ice cream, cookies, peanut butter-and-jelly sandwiches, fruit juice and some wild cereals called Fruity Pooties, Snickle Crickles or some such. At least you could put milk on it.

Our Sunday picnic, near a shallow creek, was an outstanding success, particularly since the creek contained neither shark nor octopi—a matter of great concern to Dougie. Jane Lynn, who was along, asked Dougie about his baby brother, Weebles.

"He's five months old," Dougie told her. "He's pretty worn out for a baby."

"You sure go through babies fast in your family," said Jane.

It's about an hour's drive home from our picnic spot and, although I had foresightedly stuffed their dear little mouths with chewing gum when we set out, hostilities broke out in the back seat just as we got into heavy traffic. Nini blew her top!

"How can I drive this car with you two fighting in the back seat?" I screamed, trying to be heard above the total war. "You keep that up and we'll all wind up in the hospital!

"And another thing," I howled at the top of my lungs, "if you don't stop fighting, I'm going to stop this car and spank both of you—HARD!"

"Lots of luck," said Betsy cheerfully.

A Certain No-Good Collie Dog

I am earnestly hoping that Lassie's television program will serve as a moral and spiritual inspiration to a certain no-good, frowzy, loudmouthed collie dog, name of Buster, who lives at our house. I made a big point of having Buster watch Lassie's show the other day and this was no easy task. First, I had to persuade him to leave our neighbor Miss Smith's cat, whom he had treed again. So far, thank heaven, he has never treed Miss Smith.

"Buster," I said to this bum, "Lassie is the type dog we had in mind when we adopted you. Perhaps it isn't too late for you to change your ways or, at least, try to smell a little better. It's pretty obvious from the way that little boy is hugging Lassie that she doesn't smell like a goat."

At this point in the program, Lassie was snarling at the villain. None of the people in the show were bright enough to know he was the villain, but Lassie knew right off the bat.

"See," I remarked to the leader of the Riverside Drive Cold Nose and Marching Society. "Now there is a dog who can read character. And you! Nice people like the mailman, the milkman and the laundryman, you try to tear limb from limb. But let some disreputable tramp wander down on the riverbank and he's your pal and bud. You can hardly wait to invite him home for dinner."

I had no sooner finished this part of my little pep talk when Lassie, instead of waking the little boy from a sound sleep, untied her rope and opened the window with her nose.

"Ha!" I snarled at my dog of very little brain. "You will kindly note how Lassie does not come and sneeze on sleeping people, thereby scaring them out of what's left of their wits, when she wants out in the middle of the night!"

I had a lot more to say on the subject, but it will have to wait until Lassie's next show. The big oaf went to sleep in my lap.

"I only wish," remarked my no-good collie dog, Buster, gallant leader of the Riverside Drive Cold Nose and Marching Society, "that my dear departed mother had been a police dog."

"And why, pray tell?" I inquired.

"Because with all these cops 'n robber shows making it big on TV, I would be a sensation in a whodunit I have in mind titled 'Buster Wood, Law Dog.' I could even work you in as hostess at a chi-chi gin mill called Mater's."

"I am overwhelmed with gratitude," says I. "Tell me more."

"Well, as you know, I am naturally a dashing, devil-may-care type fellow—a sort of canine Craig Stevens, you might say," explained Mr. B. with his usual modesty.

"So playing the role of a handsome, brave, smart, witty dog, who spends his life chasing criminals and fighting off lady dogs, would be no effort for me. Of course, I wouldn't fight off lady dogs too hard," he added with a lascivious smirk. "Just give 'em a bit of a chase."

"I suppose you realize that no TV whodunit even gets off the ground these days without some way-up-the-wall jazz," I reminded the dear boy.

"I thought of that and I figured the Society's own jazz combo, The Canine Cats, will make Hank Mancini sound like Lawrence Welk," said Buster. "I'll get Ruth Lyons to whip us up a theme. The kid needs a break."

"Maybe you could get her to sing with the combo and park cars in her spare time," I suggested.

"Not a chance," he replied. "I'm gonna be the star of this show and I know that dame too well. The first thing you know, I'd be parking the cars and she'd be made up as a police dog."

"May I point out that even with your crew cut, not even your dearest friends the fleas, would mistake you for a police dog," I said.

"It's true," he sighed sadly. "If only my mother had been more selective, father might not have been a sheep dog.

"Say," he said, suddenly brightening, "how about a TV show where a brave sheep dog chases cars?"

The life of my no-good collie dog, Buster, gallant leader of the Riverside Drive Cold Nose and Marching Society, has been greatly enriched since his name has appeared in the phone book. Buster has been getting a lot of mail lately.

So help me, the bulk of the mail which arrives at our house is addressed to Mr. Buster Wood. All I get are bills.

As I staggered into the house the other day, under the daily load—and I do mean mail!—Mr. B. met me.

"I've mislaid my glasses again," he said, "so you'll have to read my mail to me."

Of course, I knew he was lying in what's left of his teeth. He broke his glasses chasing Miss Smith's cat.

"Well," I began, opening an impressive-looking brochure, "here's a book club which is anxious to have the pleasure of your company as a member. They're willing to throw in a copy of *War and Peace* as an introductory offer."

"I've read it," he yawned. "So what else is new?"

"Now here's a worthy cause," I continued. "A home for unwed beagles would like a donation."

"Male or female?" he leered. "Pray proceed."

"*Life* magazine sends a message of vital importance, it says. They are willing to keep you well-informed on domestic and foreign affairs at a very friendly price," I said.

"And where would I get the friendly price?" he asked acidly.

"Look, chum, you have a liberal allowance for a dog, and what do you do with it?" I inquired.

"Well, some I spend on lady dogs, some I spend on likker and some I gamble," he explained. "The rest I spend foolishly."

I was about to open another letter when the phone rang.

"Is this the residence of Mr. Buster Wood?" asked a male voice.

"It is," I admitted.

"Is Mr. Wood at home?" he further inquired.

"He is, but he can't come to the phone at the moment," I said. "He's busy looking over his correspondence. May I take a message?"

"You may," he said graciously. "You may tell Mr. Wood that Mr. Hotzapple is calling with a special offer on storm windows."

"He doesn't need them," I told Mr. Hotzapple. "Whenever there's a storm, Mr. Wood tucks his tail between his legs and heads for the basement where he hides under the laundry tubs."

The gallant leader of the Riverside Drive Cold Nose and Marching Society curled his lip in a winning smile. Right away I knew he was up to no good.

"You will be delighted to know that still another honor has been heaped upon my handsome head," beamed my no-good collie dog, Buster. "I have been made program chairman for the annual Winter Carnival of the Riverside Drive Cold Nose and Marching Society. The choice, of course, was unanimous."

"That's nice," I replied absently, gazing at the ice-packed Ohio River in front of my house. "I suppose you're planning to engage Marian Spelman to sing 'The Star-Spangled Banner' again."

"No," said Mr. B., "she's booked to sing the national anthem and roast wieners at our Fourth of July festivity."

"At the same time?" I asked.

"For what we pay her, the least she can do is roast the wieners," he pointed out.

"You fellows drive a hard bargain," I said.

"Actually," he said coyly, "I've persuaded the members that you are the only one to fill the starring role in our Winter Carnival Historical Pageant. They wanted Ruth Lyons, but I talked them out of that idea."

"Buster," I asked suspiciously, "what are you up to?"

"Dear Girl, this role will make you famous from one end of the river to the other," he chortled. "You will recreate the stirring human drama which has torn the hearts out of millions of Americans. You will be Eliza crossing the ice!"

"I'll be WHAT?" I screamed.

"Eliza, Sweetie, and with REAL ice," he said. "As long as the river is frozen, it would be silly not to use it. And ten members of the Society, including two beagles, have volunteered to chase you across, a-snappin' at your heels."

"That is kind of them," I said frigidly.

"There is one other thing," continued Buster, warming to his subject. "To be authentic, you really should be clutching a baby as you leap across the ice. Naturally, I'd like to keep the glory in the family, so why don't you call your daughter Sally and borrow that youngest kid of hers?"

"Tell me, my fine impresario," I inquired. "While I am crossing the frozen Ohio—barefoot, undoubtedly—clutching little Betsy and hotly pursued by ten dogs, where will you be?"

"Right here, cheering you on from behind the front window," he said. "You know how I hate cold weather."

The Riverside Drive Cold Nose and Marching Society held an indignation meeting this week and Miss Ruth Lyons was the prime object of its indignation.

It seems that the membership of this august body has learned that Miss Lyons has excluded dogs from her Christmas Fund prizes, a calumny which came to light when Buster Wood, gallant leader of the group, spent ninety minutes of his valuable time waiting for the telephone to ring on Thanksgiving Day.

"We're not going to take this lying down," growled Mr. B. "We're striking a blow for dogs of all races, creeds and colors."

Buster further hinted that unless Miss Lyons saw the error of her ways and acted swiftly to rectify this sorry situation, there was a strong possibility that she would never again be crowned May Queen at the Annual Riverside Drive Cold Nose and Marching Society Spring Festival and Community Howl.

"This year we had planned to ask her to sing, despite strong opposition from several committee members," Mr. B. pointed out.

"Miss Marian Spelman is not only available but, at last hearing, hit a note four octaves higher than our finest soprano, a beagle," he added. "As a matter of fact, the note hit by Miss Spelman was so high it could only be heard by a few of the younger dogs."

Well, Ruth, don't say I haven't warned you. I told you not to fool around with the Riverside Drive Cold Nose and Marching Society. You blow that May Queen bit and you've had it. You'll never again be able to show your face at a dog show again without getting booed off the lot.

"Buster," I said, after my evening perusal of the *Post*, "the world is going to the dogs."

"And not a minute too soon," growled the gallant leader of the Riverside Drive Cold Nose and Marching Society. "The way people are running it, I'm surprised it hasn't fallen apart long ago."

"From that remark, I assume you feel you dogs could do a better job," I sniffed.

"We couldn't do much worse," said Mr. B. "The trouble with people is they just plain can't get along together. They're always yapping about peace and good will, and the next thing you know they're slinging rocks and insults."

"You refer to the recent unpleasantness in South America for Vice-President Nixon?" I asked.

"You bet I do," said Buster. "If they'd listened to me, they would have sent some famous American dog, like Lassie or Rin Tin Tin, down there on a good will tour. People don't throw rocks at dogs. Dogs are about the only thing most people really like."

"If you are implying that dog is man's best friend, how come your relations with Friendly Mailman are so strained that we still get our mail delivered next door?" I inquired. "You aren't spreading a lot of good will in that direction, old buddy."

"I love that man like a brother," lied Buster. "I tell him so every morning, loud and clear, when I rush out to greet him."

"You're loud, all right, and 'chase' would be a more apt description than 'greet,'" I said.

"See what I mean about people?" sighed Buster. "You've been a People so long, you don't even trust your own lovable collie dog who has given you and your daughter the best years of his life."

"My heart bleeds for your pitiful plight," I said. "What do you plan to run for when you dogs take over the country? I want to know in case I am forced to change my politics."

"You can come to our Cat Roast for Dogs for Democratic Action rally next week and find out," barked Mr. B. "Already, we got enough registered dogs in our organization to swing two counties. All we gotta do now is get out the vote.

"I might add," he hinted darkly, "that it would be well for you and that sassy daughter of yours to keep a civil tongue in your heads when addressing your future governor!"

"That Cleo is not a bad-looking chick, but a bit low-slung for my taste," remarked my no-good collie dog, Buster.

Mr. B.'s comments on the pulchritude of Cleo, the girl basset hound on "People's Choice," came as no surprise to me. Since Buster's hair has grown back after his recent bout with mange and he is once again a vision of loveliness, his interest in the fair sex has returned with redoubled vigor. I think the advent of spring has something to do with it, too.

"Listen, you old goat," I said, "don't get any ideas about that sweet young thing. Need I remind you that you're going on seven years old? I might also add that Cleo, rich and smart as she is, undoubtedly has every well-known dog in Hollywood chasing after her."

"The only reason I'm not a rich, well-known Hollywood dog is because I've wasted the best years of my life protecting you and that daughter of yours from the perils of Riverside Drive," sniffed Mr. B. "And what thanks do I get? Not even enough ready cash to get over the Suspension Bridge, let alone get to Hollywood and take a girl dog to a night club for a gay evening."

At this point in the argument, that dear girl boxer,

Angel, who lives next door, came waddling through the back gate for her nightly investigation of Buster's dinner left-overs.

"What a chow hound," Mr. B. sneered at the former Light of His Life.

"She's a lovely girl and kind to her family," I replied with spirit.

"Girl?" he yelped. "She'll never see seven again and, what's more, she looks sort of matronly since that last batch of puppies."

Angel's pointed ears, which miss nothing, caught Buster's snide remark about her figure.

"Cad," she growled. "And also bounder! Who was the only girl dog willing to walk down Riverside Drive with you a couple of months ago when you were known as the Covington Hairless? Ever-lovin' Angel, that's who.

"And don't give me that old Hollywood jazz, either," she added. "What girl dog in her right mind would look at you twice with Rin Tin Tin and Yukon King around."

About that time, I cut out. If there's anything I hate, it's domestic quarrels.

"What's all this jazz about Lassie's press agents giving gold medals to heroic dogs?" asked my no-good collie dog, Buster, removing his pince-nez and fixing his gimlet eye upon me.

"Had you thought of applying for this signal honor?" I inquired of the gallant leader of the Riverside Drive Cold Nose and Marching Society.

"What do I have to do?" he countered suspiciously.

"It's quite simple," I explained. "Just write them a letter telling how you are trustworthy, loyal, helpful, friendly, courteous, kind, obedient, cheerful, thrifty, brave, clean and reverent."

"I'm a dog, not a Boy Scout," protested Mr. B. "Anyway, I hate to brag."

"Whaddya mean brag?" I hollered. "The only thing you are in that list is thrifty!"

"On my allowance I have very little choice," he sniffed. "It's been months since Angel and I went dancing at Beverly Hills, and if I don't latch onto some scratch shortly, that big French poodle, Beauregarde, who thinks he's such a lady-killer, will be moving in on my territory.

"Tell me, is that there medal SOLID gold?" he asked. "The kind you can hock?"

"You don't think Lassie would be handing out brass, do you?" I said. "And anyway, they're bearing down on heroic deeds of which you ain't done none to my certain knowledge."

"Maybe they would consider what I haven't done," mused Buster. "Like I haven't chewed up any shoes since I lost my front teeth, and although I have chased cars, I have never caught one. Also I have never picked a fight with a dog smaller than I."

"Or as big," I added snidely.

"Well, nothing ventured, nothing gained," said Mr. B. "I think I'll just write a simple, modest letter telling how, when confronted with unsurmountable hazards, I rescued my Loved Ones from a cross fire of machine gun bullets when surrounded by a band of cutthroat robbers from Rabbit Hash, Kentucky, while dragging a canoe behind me."

"My memory must be failing fast," I said. "I can't seem to recall the incident."

"Don't strain yourself," urged Buster. "In return for past favors, we'll reverse our usual procedure. This time, I'll lie and YOU can swear to it!"

After attending the annual Carol Sing of the Riverside Drive Cold Nose and Marching Society, my no-good collie dog, Buster, returned to our home, Little-Tottering-on-the-Brink-of-the-Ohio, with his tail at half-mast.

"There are people out in Highland Cemetery in better health than I," he groaned.

"If I've told you once, I've told you a thousand times —lay off that Bonded Sani-Flush," I replied. "Hung over dogs get no sympathy from me."

"You have a heart of purest stone," snarled Mr. B. "And when I think of having given you the best years of my life. . . ."

"You mean you had some good ones?" I retorted acidly. "Why don't you tell me how you got yourself into this shameful condition?"

"Well, as you know, the Society gathers down on the riverbank for our caroling and this year we invited Marian Spelman to join us," said Buster. "She's a big favorite with the members, even though some of her high notes can only be heard by the younger dogs."

"Did Marian accept your kind invitation?" I inquired.

"No," explained Buster. "She sent word that she wasn't quite ready to go to the dogs."

As I pieced together the details of the merrymaking, it was clear that Marian had made a wise decision. Shortly after the carolers polished off the forty-seventh chorus of "Jingle Bells," some sore-head called the cops.

"I happened to be in very good voice," said Buster modestly. "My tenor was extremely high."

"No more so than you, apparently," said I.

After the meeting was abruptly adjourned by the constabulary, several of the members decided to go down the alley and chase cats.

"And did you join them?" I asked.

"Indeed not," Buster replied with great dignity. "Need I point out that this is the season of Peace on Earth, Good Will toward cats?"

Sometimes I think that dog is all heart!

"I hear my friend Yukon King, that brave dog who saved Sergeant Preston from so many perils of the Frozen North, is coming back to TV tonight," said Buster, who is recuperating from an auto accident in which his hind end was somewhat battered.

"Naturally, since I'm an invalid, you'll have to move the TV set to the basement," he said.

"Naturally," I replied. "And I expect you'll want me to hold your paw during the more exciting moments of the show."

"Right now, I expect you to scratch my ears, and when you've done that, run upstairs and warm a little milk to go with my Dog Yummies," ordered Mr. B. "Get on the ball, dear girl. I can always go back to the Covington Animal Hospital and my beautiful blond nurse, Wanda. She loved me madly."

"There's no fool like an old fool," I remarked. "I must say, for a dog your age, time has done nothing to dim your conceit."

"A fine Florence Nightingale you turned out to be," he growled. "You ought to turn in your lamp. Imagine, stooping to besmirch my character as I lie here on my bed of pain."

"One more night like last night and I'm going to turn in my lamp and throw in the towel, too," I said grimly. "How come, at 3:30 A.M., you get an overwhelming desire for my company?"

"Because you're handy and I'm spoiled," beamed Buster, chomping a dog biscuit. "With your attitude you'll never be like those angels of mercy I saw on 'The Nurses.'"

"And with you as a patient, I'm likely to turn up with a disposition like Ben Casey," I groaned.

"I am a poor, sick collie dog who has given you the best years of his life," said Mr. B., putting on his best poor, sick dog expression. "Anyway, this invalid bit is the best thing I've discovered so far. Wait'll I write my chum, Yukon King. The heck with mushing through snow and ice. Get yourself run over and you've got it made."

Sighing deeply, I tottered up the cellar steps to warm his milk.

"And, Sweetie," he hollered after me. "Watch the milk. It was just a mite too warm this morning."

My collie dog, Buster, gallant leader of the Riverside Drive Cold Nose and Marching Society, slept his long and happy life away while I was on vacation. He was fourteen years old and very sick and feeble.

Buster, like most collies, was a devoted dog—fiercely loyal and protective of his humans. He came to us as a puppy on my daughter Sally's twelfth birthday after I sneaked a look in her diary and read the entry: "After reading Lassie, all I want is a collie."

What I loved most about Buster was his remarkable sense of humor. Perhaps we humans endow our dogs with personalities, but I still feel that each dog has a special personality of his own.

Mr. B. was a clown, bless him, a loving, wonderful clown. He leaped for joy at the sight of Sally or me, often knocking us down in his exuberance. Once we were prone and helpless, he would lick our faces with profound affection.

"Buster," I'd holler, "with you as a friend, who needs an enemy?"

As the man of the house, Buster defended Sally and me from friends and foes alike. I recall when Sandy

Thomson, my now son-in-law, was courting Sally, that Buster was their most relentless chaperon.

"Mama," moaned Sally, charging into my bedroom one night after a date with Sandy, "I'll never get married. I'll be an old maid all my life thanks to YOUR dog!"

"He's YOUR dog, remember?" I pointed out. "And what has he done now?"

"He BIT Sandy!" groaned the future Mrs. Thomson.

"Why?" I asked. "Did Sandy offend him in any way?"

"Of course not," said Sally. "He was merely kissing me good night."

"Obviously, Buster thought Sandy was trying to bite you," I explained. "You don't know when you're well off. Be thankful you have a dog with such high moral standards and get to bed!"

Just one more story about Mr. B. . . .

One day I was going Over-the-River, as we say in Covington, and as I started up the alley to the bus stop, Buster loped ahead, ready for a brisk, stick-retrieving walk. We got to the bus stop, I boarded the bus and Buster started to board it, too.

"Go home, Buster," I ordered. "You can't get on this bus. You don't have any money."

He docilely dismounted the step, but I'll never forget the look of sheer astonishment on the bus driver's face.

How can I ever express the many ways in which Buster has enriched my life? Or thank him for those years of selfless devotion? For that overwhelming welcome when I came home? Will anyone ever be so glad to see me again?

God gives a dog only a short time on earth. But in that brief span, if you're lucky enough to have a dog like

Buster, you will never know such wondrous, undemanding love.

So good-by, darling Mr. B., and thank you for those fourteen happy years. I loved you very much.